THE
False Sense of Urgency
AND HOW TO
#WINtheNOW

Eric Recker, DDS

WESTBOW
PRESS®
A DIVISION OF THOMAS NELSON
& ZONDERVAN

WestBow Press books may be ordered through booksellers or by contacting:

WestBow Press
A Division of Thomas Nelson & Zondervan
1663 Liberty Drive
Bloomington, IN 47403
www.westbowpress.com
844-714-3454

ISBN: 978-1-6642-2984-6 (sc)
ISBN: 978-1-6642-2985-3 (e)

Print information available on the last page.

WestBow Press rev. date: 05/11/2021

Acknowledgements

I thank God from the bottom of my heart for planting the seed to write early on in the pandemic. All I have is from Him and all I own is His. He doesn't need me to write, but He asked me to be obedient and gave me the words, and I pray these words will be used for great impact.

My beautiful wife, Amy Recker. I way outkicked my coverage. I married up. Way up. If everyone had an Amy Recker in their life, the world would simply be a better place. She is unconditionally loving and supportive of me and my wild ideas. We have shared life for twenty-seven years, and I hope and pray for many more.

My sons, Blake and Jace. You challenge me to be the best version of myself, and I am so thankful for the adventures we get to share. I love you guys more than I ever thought I could!

My family. My parents, Mark and Linda, and my siblings, Bryan and Hillary. Thanks for providing love, wisdom, and guidance. And my in-laws, the Hetlands. I married up in the in-law department as well.

My inner circle. You know who you are. Stan, Todd, Kevin, Steve, and Matt. I love you guys. You all mean so much to me.

My team at Recker Dental Care—Jeanna, Lori, Kaitlyn, Linda, Leigh, Debbie, Deb, Heather, Kenzie, Jana, Abbi, Emily, Kim, Marla, Bailey, Kara, and Josh. You have all watched me dream about so many things over the years and have loved and supported me well.

I am missing a ton of people, but you know who you are, and the acknowledgments can't be a book in themselves. God bless all of you.

Preface

On March 17, 2020, I furloughed my dental team. I sent them home with no clue when I could welcome them back. We closed up shop to everything except emergencies. It was surreal. It was agonizing. It was stressful. It created tremendous fear and uncertainty. I hated it. I cried. I felt sorry for myself. I lamented the loss of life as we had known it.

But did I really? A breakneck pace of life for the last eighteen years of dental practice, overloaded and compounded by running the business, keeping track of eighteen employees, and being involved in several extracurricular activities. And by extracurricular activities, I mean triathlon to Ironman, climbing Kilimanjaro, dental missions to Haiti and Guatemala, riding my bike across Iowa in a day three times as a fundraiser (because two times isn't enough), the Leadville 100 MTB race. And, oh, by the way, trying to be a father, husband, friend, and my own best version.

In the midst of the pause I was faced with, this break from business as usual, a spark was lit that there might be something more to this life than going from stress to stress. And the idea to write was born. Little did I know what I was in for in the way of self-awareness and self-discovery. And in a key conversation, the idea for *The False Sense of Urgency* was born.

I think the false sense of urgency is a very real thing, and it is wreaking havoc on our hearts and our minds and in many cases crushing our very souls. It is that constant nagging of "what's next," of "nothing is good enough." Of "I should be doing more." And it is exaggerated and exacerbated by our phones and constant need to be plugged in and in the know. It is made worse by comparison culture and feelings and rumblings that the grass may be greener elsewhere.

The false sense takes and takes. It stokes our worry, fear, stress, and anxiety, leaving us a shell of our best selves, with a constant feeling of needing to do something and at the same time paralyzed by inactivity and analysis paralysis. It is relentless and it is real, but it does not have to be our only reality.

We can take back some ground in this fight! Join me as we learn about the false sense of urgency, share a few stories here and there, and learn in the end how to #WINtheNOW and take back that lost ground and take back our lives. We get one shot at this life, so let's live it to the fullest!

Introduction

Who likes quizzes? Answer: absolutely no one. But here's the thing. We need to know where we start to know where we want to go or something clichéd like that. So just humor me and take the quiz. Simple yes or no will do for each question (except for number 4).

1. Do you lie awake with your head spinning but can't pinpoint the next action step?
2. Do you keep yourself busy with busywork but never seem to accomplish anything?
3. Do you always feel like the next big thing is about to go down but you are completely unprepared?
4. Did COVID-19 cause you to relax because you had some time off or a different schedule, or did it get your head spinning even more?
5. Do you have a constant low- to mid-grade anxiety that follows you everywhere you go?
6. Are you a "well, he/she just can't sit still" type? Has anyone ever said this about you?
7. Has anyone ever told you to just sit, relax, and enjoy for a little bit?
8. Are you a Mary (answer no) or a Martha (answer yes)?
9. Do you ever look at an upcoming event thinking there simply won't be enough time to get all the things done that you want to get done?
10. Is time slipping through your fingertips, and do you feel helpless to stop it?

So how did you do? More yeses than nos? I suspect that at least a few of these struck a chord with you. What we are poking at here is the false sense of urgency. That nagging sense that more needs to be done without really putting your finger on what it is. That sensation that says what you have done is not enough and that there should have been more. This mind-spinning feeling. This can't-sit-still feeling. That I-have-so-much-to-do-even-though-I-know-I-actually-don't feeling. If you are intrigued, I invite you to read on. If you are not intrigued, at least give me a couple of chapters to make my case. There's really something here for everyone. I suspect you won't be disappointed.

Chapter 1

THE FALSE SENSE
OF URGENCY

In everyday life there is always
manana. There is no urgency.

—*Mark Spitz*
nine-time Olympic champion

I t's that nagging feeling in the pit of your stomach. That thing that makes you wake up from a deep sleep and requires immediate attention—or so it seems. It's that low-grade rumbling that never really lets you unwind, never lets you fully relax. It is a full-on demand of your resources—time, energy, and talents—but with no end game. In fact, if I asked you to answer why to this sense of urgency, you probably couldn't tell me. It becomes your master, and you are its puppet. It prevents rest. It tells you that you need to look at your phone x times per day. And x is a big number in this case. Did you just put your phone down? Doesn't matter. Better pick it back up and check again. It tells you that you'd better hit your phone routine one more time.

I suspect we all have a phone routine. You pick up your phone and run through the usual things before you put it back down. And you'd better get it done quickly. You have very little time before your next patient, meeting, dinner with family, call, Zoom meeting, or whatever.

It is what keeps you from sitting down and actually relaxing because there is too much to do. (What in the world is relaxing anyway?) It keeps you unsatisfied, always feeling like something is missing. But you can't pinpoint what is missing. You sure try. But the reality is there is no time because you have all these *things* to do but get paralyzed into inactivity by the false sense of urgency. It is driving you toward burnout. Take a moment or two to ponder that. It is. And you know it, but you can't quite put your finger on it.

You are a bit blinded by it, but deep down, you are restless. Unsettled. Because there is more to do. *Much* more to do. What is there that *has* to be done? You really can't even answer that question, but it has to be done. So you come in early and you stay late, and you really aren't very good at using your time, so you have no satisfaction of accomplishment. And you need to go home. Or now, since there is a good chance you work at home, you need to step out of your office and back into life with your family. But there is always one more thing.

Since there is no drive and you are right there, you justify a little more time in front of the computer to zone out. But only after picking up your phone for two to forty-five minutes, getting lost in social media and maybe a few videos that link to other videos courtesy of clickbait and those link to other articles all created to give you fear, worry, anxiety, and stress. And then you really need to get with your family because it is past time to eat. And since your mind is spinning fast enough to make you fall off your chair from all the garbage you digested on your phone just now, your mind is truly and fully elsewhere, and you have no ability to be present for your family or your spouse. Or if you live alone, you know you may just go back to the phone, Netflix, Vudu, Hulu, Jobu, or whichever fix you choose.

And you really didn't get those last few work tasks done, so you either can't fall asleep because you are thinking about them or you wake up in the night thinking about them. Either way, good luck. Good luck falling asleep. Or good luck getting back to sleep. Who needs sleep anyway? Five hours a night has been plenty for me all my life since I can remember. But is it really enough? The answer is no. And it really catches up to you over time.

So it all spirals. Day after day. We wake up saying, "Today will be different," but we really don't change anything. And if all our inputs are the same, why would we expect any kind of significant change? You will only make improvements to the degree that you will try new approaches. We need to change some inputs. Redirect, midcourse correct, or all-out pivot to try to kick this thing out of our lives for good.

Imagine a day in which you wake up refreshed. You do your thing all day undistracted as much as that is even possible. You take a little time to breathe at lunch. Then you get back at it full on in the afternoon and then efficiently tie up a few loose ends at work or at home. Then you step away to be fully present with whatever you have left after a workday without a cloud hanging over your head.

This is possible, but it won't come as easily as you are hoping. However, despite that news, please read on. A few basic inputs can have a profound response. A minor tweak here and there can change your course significantly. Rome wasn't built in a day and all of that, and you must remember that this false sense of urgency has been bothering you for a long time. Most people have no clue they fight it. But once you are aware, you really can't remember when you didn't have it.

We get addicted to it. And I do not know of a single treatment for addiction that takes minutes or even hours. It is a process, but it is a process in which you can see tangible results very quickly. I always like things that give me some results right away. Just like a cleanse gives you a jump start, let's look at this book as sort of a cleanse with some maintenance going forward.

This is a good time for a disclaimer. I am *not* a mental-health professional in any way, shape, or form. I am just a person trying to recover from a life governed by the false sense of urgency who wants to help you do the same. If you need to see a mental health professional, please do not hesitate. Many great therapists and counselors are available. Addiction is serious business. *Really* serious. But there is hope. There is the chance to overcome.

While we are here in this introductory chapter, let me share another analogy for the false sense of urgency. I am a pilot. More about that later. But a month ago, I needed to undergo a biannual flight review with a flight instructor. Jake went up with me, and what I love about Jake is that he is superinterested in me surviving while flying. My wife and my family also like that about him. We went through a bunch of maneuvers and scenarios and had some great discussions.

One of the exercises was for me to wear glasses that only allow me to see the instrument panel in the plane. So I put my head down and closed my eyes, and Jake maneuvered the plane in any number of directions for what felt like several minutes. Then he paused. He wanted me to tell him which way we were headed. I said we were gaining altitude and tracking to the right. Then he said to open my eyes and correct it. We were rapidly descending and tracking left. I was completely disoriented!

That is a perfect picture of the false sense of urgency and what it does to us. We get disoriented very quickly. We have thoughts in our heads about what we need to do and where we need to go and all the things we need to do. But we get overwhelmed and lose our bearings, and quite frankly, we suffer the effects of it. We have to correct before we crash. If I had delayed too long in the direction we were heading, I would have crashed. Jake wouldn't have let that happen in our flight review, but Jake doesn't fly with me every time.

Another way to frame this concept is to consider the illusion of action. The feeling you need to do something when staying the course. And being patient, in this case, is the right course. You don't need to act. You need to be patient. Staying the course, in some situations, is all you need to do.

I need to learn to get my bearings so I can be a safe pilot, and we need to get our bearings so we don't get snowed under by this thing called the false sense of urgency. We do that by recognizing it and fixing it. It's not that easy, but it is doable, and we will talk a *lot* about it in the upcoming pages, so please stick with me! I think it will be worth your time!

If you will allow me, let's take this journey. Let's walk down this path. If I am wrong about any of the points in this book, I apologize. But you are only out the price of this book and the time you took to read it. I suspect the book will be worth it. Even if you only grab a few pearls and some self-awareness, your time will be well spent. After all, that is what reading books is all about. Try to grab a few ideas from each book that resonate and are applicable to your life. I welcome your comments. Please email me at falseurgency@gmail.com.

Chapter 2

NO MAN IS AN ISLAND

The life of a solitary man will be certainly miserable, but not certainly devout.

—*Samuel Johnson*

N o man is an island. This line is from a sermon by the poet John Donne. We as human beings depend on each other; we say, "You can't do this all by yourself. You can't manage this all by yourself." The entirety of the quote by Donne is this: "No man is an island, entire of self; every man is a piece of the continent, a part of the main."

We are not completely self-sufficient despite a card catalog of books that attempt to suggest otherwise. (A card catalog, for those who are thirty-five or under, is a dinosaur of sorts in the library for organizing book titles. And while we are at it, a library is a place where books are kept). Needless to say, there have been a lot of books about self-sufficiency and being a self-made human.

The fact of the matter is that we are better together. We need each other, as seen on the T-shirts of Many Hands for Haiti, the words *Pibon Ansanm*, which is creole for Better Together. Many Hands for Haiti is a group I am thrilled to be a part of. They are a nonprofit group that is focused on the first thousand days of the lives of children in Haiti, ensuring their nutrition and health and setting them up for success later in life. And as the children are blessed with a good start to life, families are blessed as well. This is not a handout group and the goal is for all of this to become sustainable. And we are headed in that direction! I am blessed to serve on their board and having been to Haiti half a dozen times, better together is where it's at. It is a beautiful concept and a wonderful organization. Please take some time to visit www. MH4H.org to see the work they are doing if you are interested.

We are seeing in this pandemic just how dangerous it is for us to be isolated from others. The mental health toll is catastrophic. I fear that some may never fully recover to become the best version of themselves. Isolation can lead to horrific things, such as suicide and abuse. We simply need each other. And in these times, we have had to be creative to find ways to connect—Zoom, FaceTime, Skype—all the tools that grandparents or parents with family far away know all too well. It is just not the same as face to face, but it is light years better than nothing. You can see emotions. You can see smiles, sadness, loneliness. We can't even see those emotions at the store with all our masks on, but through technology, we can see each other. A phone call is fine, but the data is limited. We need to see each other! We really are better together!

What I am really poking at here is surrounding yourself with a group of people that I would call your trusted advisors. Your inner circle. Your crew. In most cases, I would suspect that your group of trusted advisors don't even all know each other, but they have you in common. And be careful when choosing who you let in here. These need to be the right kind of people for you. No *energy vampires*, as Jon Gordon would say. If you haven't read any of his books, do yourself a favor and dive in (right after you finish this one). You don't need people who are negative and drag you down. This is your inner circle, your choice of your own personal board of directors. And they have one thing in common: helping you become the best you.

So how do you go about choosing these people for your inner circle? Well, here are a few disqualifiers. These cannot be energy vampires, as I previously mentioned. You don't need that in your life. They cannot be people who suck the life out of you and try to borrow your energy and leave you with nothing in return. You have no obligation to anyone to ask them into this group. You get to be selfish here. You *have to* be selfish here. If you dread a text or a snap or any kind of communication or message when you see it pop up from them and you think in your mind, *What now?* then they are not eligible. In fact, you may want to consider whether there is value in any kind of relationship with this person.

If the person you are considering is selfish or self-focused, then that's also a no, because how can they help you navigate life if they are focused only on theirs and can't wait to shift the conversation to their concerns? If this person is known or observed to be a gossip or cannot keep others' confidence, then no! Avoid! If you have heard someone say, "I wasn't supposed to share this, but …"

then you just have to assume they will do the same thing with the personal information you share in confidence with them.

Do you dread seeing this person or spending time with them one on one but are okay with them in a group? If so, then another obvious no. Do they always have ulterior motives, always trying to get something for themselves for "helping" you? These are just a few things to consider when seeking your group of trusted advisors.

And while we are on this topic, maybe now is a good time to take stock of any toxic relationships you have and determine if they are fixable. What I mean by fixable is this: Can this relationship become mutually beneficial? If not, maybe it's time for a "blessed subtraction." You can only exist and move forward with so many people pulling you down. For every relationship in which someone is pulling you down with their stuff, you need several that are lifting you up. So how's your balance here? And are you always the one pulling up others? So evaluate. Take a little time and really evaluate your relationships. And know it is okay to pull back from a toxic relationship. We have to guard our hearts.

You will often find that these toxic relationships were with a narcissistic person anyway and you were putting forth most of the effort to prop them up. That is *exhausting*! Let them go and prey on someone else, or better yet, be honest with them—if you are willing to have that conversation. Maybe they will go on to be a better version of themselves. Just be tactful about it.

Okay, now the more important part. How do you pick your inner circle? How do you form your group of trusted advisors? How many is enough? These will be people you want to be in contact with regularly, so if it becomes a burden to stay in contact with everyone regularly, you may have overshot. As an example, here is my inner circle.

My lovely wife Amy.

A great friend, Kevin, that I met through a mutual friend at the start of the pandemic. We just hit it off. He challenges me. And I like to be challenged.

Next is Todd, a friend and fellow entrepreneur whom I have known since high school. We have lunch every Tuesday and talk about owning our businesses, loving our families well, and baseball cards.

My mentor, Stan, towers over me at 6'8". That is a rarity for me. I am 6'5", so literally looking up to someone is a bit uncommon.

Steve was a year ahead of me in dental school. He was assigned to be my Big Brother as far as dental school is concerned. We have taken classes and received advanced degrees together. I respect him immensely. We have great talks.

And my sensei and broheim, Matt, who is also my management consultant for my dental practice. But much more than that; he is a wonderful friend and simply one of the best dudes you would be lucky enough to meet.

That's my crew.

I have many other friends and family whom I love dearly and feel comfortable confiding in, but these are my six. And six is a good number for me. We are all reciprocal. We do life well together. We encourage each other. We pray for each other. We celebrate together, and we mourn together. We strengthen each other. I could show up on any of their doorsteps at 3:00 a.m., and I would be graciously welcomed with open arms, no questions asked (at least as gracious as someone could be woken up at 3:00 a.m.). I am blessed by these people.

So that is my group. I have chosen people who

> I look forward to spending time with
> have wisdom that challenges me
> I have great and challenging conversations with
> I fully trust with any of the details big or small in my life
> have no ulterior motives
> want to be their best self and help me become my best self

If you are a relatively introverted person this may seem overwhelming to you. If you are extroverted, you may be thinking how it might be possibly to limit it to six. There is no magic in the number six. It is a number. It happens to be my number. Two could be a good number. Six could be a good number. This is your journey. It is not someone else's journey. But you need, at an absolute bare minimum, one other human. You simply can't do life alone and thrive.

Another note. These people didn't just come to me saying they wanted to be in my inner circle, my group of trusted advisors. It required a little effort. I asked Todd if he wanted to start having lunch. That was about sixteen years ago. I reached out to Stan to ask if he would be my mentor. I felt as if I didn't have a mentor in my life, and I wanted to have someone who had done more life than I had and had gleaned some wisdom from that life. And I hired Matt to help my practice, but I count it amongst the best money I have ever spent, as it has become much more than a business relationship. And Amy is Amy. She is fabulous. I am so blessed to have met her in 1993 at a bowling alley. I know—classy. She is just fantastic.

So now you have some work to do. Please do not just race to the next chapter. I would like to have you write down the names of ten people you know at least fairly well. Just any ten names, maybe the ten you know the best. Then look at those names through the lens of this chapter. Think on it—undistracted thinking, not just letting it run on the back burner while you check your phone. And certainly think of someone who might be your mentor, someone who has been there and done that and lived some life.

I think most people would be honored (and possibly terrified) to be asked to be a mentor. Those same people would probably have no idea what it means to be a mentor, but that puts them in the perfect place of humility to be a mentor. This person doesn't have to be older than you; the point is that they are someone you look up to or have seen their life and you want to learn from them and their experiences.

So make the list. Refine the list. Tell people about this chapter and that you want them to be on your team. Exciting days are ahead if you find your team and start to do life with them.

Chapter 3

WHAT IS TRULY IMPORTANT (TIME)

Time is what we want most,
but what we use worst.

—William Penn

t really doesn't matter who you are and what you do and how busy you are. We are all governed by the same law of time. The same twenty-four-hour clock. No dollar amount can change that. It is nonnegotiable. There is not yet a way to buy more time, and I suspect there never will be. Ask a parent as their child moves out of the house and into college what they would like more of: the answer is typically time. Ask a dying person what they want more of (especially one dying early from cancer). It certainly won't be money. It is time. Ask grandparents as they are saying goodbye to kids and grandchildren after a visit on a Sunday afternoon what they want more of. I suspect it would be time.

It really makes no difference how much more you want time. You can't have it. You get twenty-four hours each day. And in that twenty-four hours you must sleep. Seven hours or more would be great. And you have to get ready in the morning and get ready for bed at night, so let's say you have sixteen usable hours in a day. How will you use them?

A workday may be pretty obvious in how you use them, although it may look a bit different, as many who went into a physical office space are now finding themselves working from home. Your day may be like my days—fully scheduled in fifteen-minute blocks with patients. I know what I will be doing all day, but it may also be discretionary for you, and you may have tasks you need to accomplish, but you may work on other things if you get those done. You may be a CEO/CFO/COO, manager, etc., with a day full of meetings and emails. You may be a stay-at-home mom with a cazillion (yes, that's a number, and yes, it's a big number) interruptions and distractions. And it is all okay. It is part of your journey. Not someone else's, yours. So let's dive in a little deeper and see what is worthy of our sixteen hours.

Many of you know the story of Mary and Martha. This is not meant to be anything more than a story of how time is used for illustration purposes. It just happens to be from the Bible. It is from Luke 10:38–42. Jesus and his disciples had come to Martha's house. They all went in and Martha's sister Mary sat near Jesus's feet and learned from his teachings, as likely everyone else in the house did as well. But Martha was distracted and enthralled by the big dinner she was preparing all alone. She was frustrated and felt it was unfair Mary was not helping her with all of the preparations. So she tattled on Mary to Jesus. Jesus said to her, "Martha, you are worried and upset over all of these details. There is only one thing worth being concerned about. Mary has discovered it and it will not be taken from her."

So there it is, and this may ring true for some of us. Before I go any further, this is not meant to be shaming in any way. Just an observation. Again, here it is: the mom who spends the whole weekend that her kids are home preparing food when she really wants to spend time with her kids. Her heart is absolutely in the right place, but then her kids are gone, and what did she miss out on? A lot. How about the party planner who has an event on the calendar at their house and struggles and strives for every detail, and then all of a sudden, the party is over and they didn't even enjoy it?

How about the guy who put together the hundred-page COVID-19 response plan just to have it torn apart by a governor's mandate and then has to start over? (Oh wait, that was me. Yes, guilty as charged. I am that guy.) How about the executive, manager so buried by email that they never get much past answering and satisfying their inbox because they have never set any boundaries with their time? How about the relentless "yes" volunteer that is at everything helping out and never misses an opportunity to be on a committee or be at an event but quietly loses their family and relationships along the way because of lack of presence. There are countless examples here and I could list more.

To the mom slaving away with food, may I graciously suggest ordering pizza or having everyone help with meal prep? It's okay, I promise. They love your food, but they also love you and want to see you. Order the pizza—maybe even use paper plates and cups so there is little to no cleanup—and get back to just hanging out, which I suspect is what you really want to do anyway. To the party planner, it is okay. The party won't be perfect, and it doesn't have to be. But if your focus is on perfection, you will miss relationship every time. And to the volunteer, thank you for your willingness to help out, but other people need to take a turn. Your people are missing you, and they also want some of your time. But we need to allow ourselves grace to realize it is okay not to cook every meal. It is okay to plan and let the party happen. It is okay to set boundaries on email. If you don't set boundaries, I promise, no one else will.

For me, it is a head that never stops spinning. I tend to pick up my phone just to numb out or zone out for a while. To basically put my brain on idle and get a little burst of dopamine. But then I hang out in that space for way too long.

While we are here, let's look at phones a little bit. Let's poke at this phone thing. I know, this is a hot-button issue, and people get ludicrously defensive about their phones. I assure you, I have heard the excuses, and I have used all of the excuses. And that's all they are: excuses.

Never before in history have we been so connected. Never before have we had such power at our fingertips. We literally have what would have been considered a supercomputer a short few years ago right at our disposal (memories flash of my Commodore 64 and floppy disks). Never before have we had the ability to become so instantly and profoundly distracted so quickly, so powerfully, so subtly, so insidiously. I could probably write a book on phones, but we would have to put ours down to read it, or we might even read or listen to the book on our phones. What a world we live in! So let's cover a few basics.

Screen time: the great equalizer. It's simply that. How much time is your phone unlocked? How much time are you on your phone? It's a harsh reality when we consider how a big chunk of our sixteen hours is spent on our phones. And if you have the fruit brand of phone (iPhone), which most of us do, you can break it down to *social media* (social networking, such a fancy distortion of reality), *productivity*, and *other*. You can even see the apps that suck the most time and are used the most on your phone. And if you are an Android user, you can use an app such as RescueTime to track the same metrics.

So if we have sixteen hours in a day, what happens if we have spent four of those hours on our phones? And, let's be honest here: What have we gotten back in exchange for those 4 hours? Is Facebook your favorite time suck? Pinterest? Instagram? Twitter? ESPN? Snapchat? Games? YouTube? News apps? Pick your poison, and watch the hours add up. Five minutes here and there add up really quick if the five minutes is used every ten minutes. That's pretty easy math.

You could even argue phones have simply subbed in for TV and magazines, the brain candy of the previous generations. Or even consider the romance or trashy novels of yesterday. You might be even considered an academic for reading them these days as they involve opening a book.

Big time disclaimer here: I am not trying to judge you or be self-righteous here. Anyone is welcome to see my screen time. I am just as guilty, just as distracted. Honestly. I promise I am not judging but rather trying to help. If you are feeling judged, may I humbly suggest that the feeling welling up inside you may be more conviction than judgment? It is not a good feeling to realize we may be sabotaging ourselves. Doing something that simply isn't helping us.

May I again humbly suggest that if you are spending hours of time on your phone while at the same time feeling as if you have no time, something has to give, and it is probably your phone time. It is hard to put it down, but this I do know: you simply cannot be present and be on your phone at the same time. The two are mutually exclusive. You either get to be fully present where you are, or fully distracted by your phone. You can't do both. You are in La La Land on your phone, and any conversation you are having, is, to put it bluntly, total junk. I know this. Believe me. I have tried. I have justified being on my phone at dinner. I have convinced myself it doesn't matter if I am on my phone while we are watching a show or a movie. And what happens next—my kids are on their phones and the only person paying any attention is Amy, my better half. My beautiful wife can live life without her phone much better than the Recker boys and their father can.

Well, you are just trading one screen for another, and that may very well be true, but when all four of us watch a show or a movie, we are interacting with each other, together, talking about the show together. We may even pause it to share something from our day. That seems to happen a lot at our house. We are watching a show and we pause it because someone remembers a highlight from the day and we talk about it. I love that, but it doesn't happen with phones in all of our hands.

The bottom line is that unless intentionally for work-related purposes (and you must be cautious here, because we all know that even doing work on our phones, social media, shopping, news, etc., are only one click away), phones are still time-suckers. I know it for a fact. My life has demonstrated it. I think you know it as well. So just be conscious of it. As GI Joe said, "Knowing is half the battle." Sometimes, as you go to pick up your phone, consider if it is worth picking up. Is it worth being distracted? Is what you are going to look at really more important than anything else going on in the room?

Self-awareness of the false sense of urgency present in your life is huge. I am forty-three, and I just really put my finger on it this year. I am now finally aware of it and trying my best to learn to manage it. For my sake. For my brain's sake. For the sake of my friends and loved ones whom I spend time with.

What about watching TV? What about binge watching Netflix or Hulu or Vudu or YouTube TV or YouTube? It's really no different than lingering on our phones. Did you know that there are social media algorithms that also exist on streaming services that are designed to get you never to leave? Kind of like the line in the Eagles song, "Hotel California." You can check out any time you like, but you can never leave. Sooner or later, you have spent (or wasted) three hours, and now what? Your to-do list still looks the same, and you are mentally fried from what you have been taking in. And what about all the ads that appear when you are searching or scrolling. Eerily, those ads seem to be hand selected for you. They are, all part of the elaborate scheme to get you to consume and spend money and never put down your phone.

Try watching the documentary *The Social Dilemma* if you really want to see how much of a puppet we are in all of this. Just recently, I had a conversation with someone about a product I had never searched for on my phone. My phone was, however, in my pocket and locked. The next time I unlocked my phone and looked at Facebook, there was an ad for that product we had just discussed. Yikes! That's more than a little scary!

What about news? Talk about an avenue for creating a false sense of urgency. Media is about fear. Say what you want. We all walk a fine line between being informed and being scared out of our ever-living minds. People are drinking the Kool-Aid, and fear is off the charts. I have chosen not to watch the news because I know what it does to me. It kills my joy. I know the kind of anxiety I have when I watch it, so for the last year since the pandemic started, I haven't. You may say that I have my head in the sand, but the last 12 months have shown me if there is something I need to hear about, it will make its way to my social media feed or even more likely someone will share it with me. So I am not missing out on much, except for the fear. I also subscribe to dental practice–related email blasts that inform me of the stuff that actually affects my profession. So I hear about it, but just don't let it dominate my mind multiple times a day.

So I don't have my head in the sand. I just know my limitations, and news is not good for me. It causes me to get all amped up.

It is overly sensational and getting worse by the day. It is not necessarily resembling anything that is actually accurate, no matter what side of the aisle you find yourself. In fact, the entire business model of media is fear and anger. That's what they are selling! Don't hear what I am not saying. You may watch the news. You don't need my blessing. You just have to count the cost and see what that consumption is doing to you and those around you. If you find yourself to be sort of a negative person and you watch a lot of news, maybe cut back a little and see what happens. We only get sixteen hours.

What about online shopping or Pinterest or any number of other apps? What about reading books on your kindle or e-reader or phone or tablet? Again, these can be good things, but it is vital to get a feel for the bigger picture and how much of your time they are consuming (or how much of your time you are allowing them to consume).

What about drive time to work? I know this has changed a lot with COVID-19. Many people who had a long commute find themselves with a ten-second commute across the hall. I talked to a patient who starts her day from home at about 3:30 a.m., and then she is done by noon or one and goes to play golf. She is super happy! Who knows what will happen in the future if this work from home trend will continue. In any event, what are you doing with your drive time? Zoning out? Zoning out to music? Listening to the news or to videos from social media? How are you using that time? What about listening to some positive podcasts from people like Jon Gordon, Bob Goff, or Dave Ramsey's EntreLeadership or Graham Cooke's Brilliant TV? If you are stuck with this time, you might as well learn something.

Or what about simply some quiet, unplugged, undistracted time for your brain to rest or to be free to think about whatever? What about just breathing? What about a call to catch up with a friend you haven't talked with for in a while, just to catch up? And guess what. You have an out. when you get home, you need to hang up!

The thing is that we all have all these things to do with our sixteen hours, and they spin in our minds, but we get distracted so easily, we spin into inaction, and we zone out and spend more and more time on our phones and fill our discretionary time more and more, and as we end up losing that time, our heads spin even more! And the false sense of urgency gets even worse. There has to be a better way.

Our sixteen hours are what we have. And we have relationships that need to be nurtured and tasks to get done and meetings to go to and sporting events and maybe an impromptu conversation that needs to be had with a spouse or child or parent. We need to be available for these things. And if we are lost in the false sense of urgency or glued to our phones, we will miss it. This is our lives. We get one shot. Do we want to look back on it and see that all we have to show for ourselves is screen time and a bunch of stuff we don't need?

So what is productive time and what is unproductive time? That's a great question. And one I don't have a great answer for. The point is this- sometimes the best time has nothing to show for it in concrete terms. Sometimes it is just time to be. Time to rest. Time to invest in relationships. Time to live. Time to love. Time to not worry about the next task at hand.

You will get to discover what is productive and what is not. But remember this- you do not have to show anything concrete for time to be productive. Restful time is incredibly productive. It gives your life meaning and flavor. It renews your energy for the journey ahead. And time that seems productive when you are really just spinning your wheels and need to take a pause but you won't- is that time productive? There are no right or wrong answers here. Just a different way of thinking. We only get sixteen hours.

Chapter 4

SELF-AWARENESS (I.E., I KNOW THERE IS A PROBLEM. NOW WHAT?)

Self-awareness gives you the capacity to learn from your mistakes as well as your successes. It enables you to keep growing.

—*Lawrence Bossidy*

S elf-awareness is a tough but important concept. It is important to know yourself. After all, no one spends more time with you than you. You are aware (or soon will be) of your own routines—the foods you like, the situations that make you thrive and those that crush you with anxiety. You should also be aware of the people around you who build you up as well as those who tear you down.

I am finally starting to develop self-awareness in my forties. I started doing triathlon in 2006. I like to say that either I am a recovering triathlete or that I did triathlon in a former life. Triathlon fit me well, too well. And I think you will see why.

I bought a bike on a Friday afternoon at my local bike shop in June of 2006. It was my first road bike (think skinny tires and curved handlebars). The next day there was an Olympic distance triathlon in my hometown. I got up Saturday morning and biked the Olympic distance triathlon bike course (25 miles), ran a 5 km on Sunday (3.1 miles, which I already could do), and swam 500 meters on Monday. I actually had to ask the person who worked at the pool how many laps equaled 500 m. The conversation went something like this- "Hey, how many laps do I need to swim for 500 meters?" Answer- "Ten." Jump in the pool. Swim ten laps. Get out of the pool. Good. Ten weeks later, I completed my first sprint distance triathlon (500-meter swim, 12-mile bike, 5 km run). Four weeks later, I completed my second sprint triathlon. The next summer, my first Olympic distance triathlon (1500 m swim, 25-mile bike, and 10 km run), the next year, my first half-ironman distance (1.2-mile swim, 56-mile bike, half marathon- 13.1 miles). After I finished the half-Ironman race (also known as 70.3 for the total distance in miles), I made my wife swear never to let me do that distance again, let alone a longer one. I told her this as I sat at the finish line completely smoked from five and a half hours of swimming, biking, and running, with legs that felt like lead and were fighting a war of which would seize up in a cramp next.

She didn't keep her end of the bargain. Truth be told, I wouldn't let her keep her end of the bargain. Several more 70.3 races later, I found myself toeing the line for two full Ironman races, one in the fall of 2010 and one in the summer of 2011. An Ironman day is a long day. You have to finish in less than seventeen hours to hear the words at the finish line. And they were oh so sweet. "Eric Recker, you are an Ironman!" One of the most treasured pieces of advice I ever received before my first Ironman race was this- It is a long day. Something will go wrong. That advice rang true when my GPS watch, which also doubled as my run pace and bike computer, drifted to the bottom of the intercoastal waterway in Wilmington, North Carolina, five minutes into Beach to Battleship, my first Ironman race. The mass swim start (everyone starts at the same time) for a triathlon looks similar to the koi pond at the zoo at feeding time. Bodies kicking and swimming over other bodies and you take some unintentional body blows. Eleven hours later, I crossed the finish line wearing my wife's pink Timex watch. Something had went wrong. It was a long day. It was ok.

I finished those races. I finished Ironman Coeur D'Alene in just under twelve hours less than nine months after Beach to Battleship. I somehow got a blister on my foot during the bike portion (how does that even happen?) and ran a marathon with a blister on the bottom of my foot. It is a long day. Something went wrong. I have only done a couple of short triathlons since. It turns out the finish line for me wasn't worth the twenty-plus hours of training per week, on top of being a dad, husband, dentist, board member, and friend. I wear many hats. We all do.

I actually stopped racing because I couldn't stand the thought of ten workouts per week anymore. I couldn't bear driving to the pool three mornings per week to go back and forth, back and forth, for ninety minutes. I couldn't bear the thought of a six-hour bike ride every single week. And I was sick of waking up at 3:00 a.m. on Wednesdays to run for two to three hours—before a full day of work. I think it comes down to willpower. It is a finite resource. And when we realize this, we have to stare it down. I knew I was torched on triathlon when I crossed the finish line in Coeur D'Alene in 2011, but it wasn't until I completed the Leadville 100 MTB (mountain bike) ride in 2017 that I realized the finish wasn't worth the training.

Willpower is such a finite resource. It doesn't matter your sport or your activity interests. I have talked to people who do CrossFit, body building, swimming, running, biking, rucking, etc. and they all have mentioned willpower and long-term ability to keep at it in their chosen activity. And my willpower was all but gone.

The Leadville 100 MTB is a 100-mile mountain bike ride, all more than 9,000 feet above sea level. And the finish line simply wasn't worth it. And the amazing thing is that the week of the race, I knew the finish line wouldn't be enough.

But that was huge! I learned that it was okay to step away from racing even though that was who I was. That's the number-one thing people would ask of me: *When's the next race, Eric?* Over and over. Because it defined me. Would I change anything? Nope. But now I know, so I don't sign up for races anymore. I still love exercising and riding my bike. It is just different now.

The false sense of urgency keeps you at redline—you know, that line on your car's RPM gauge. What happens if the needle stays right at the redline or, even worse, exceeds it? What are the consequences? Damage. The engine blows up. You probably are going too fast. The bottom line is this: it is not sustainable. That is why the line is there. To be cautious. To avoid it. To stay below it.

Sure, there are redline events and redline times in our lives. But if there are redline seasons where, as Amy says, you are going 170 mph all the time, you simply can't sustain that. Even Formula 1 or NASCAR vehicles can't sustain it. They need to pit, refuel, take a break. You are done with the race altogether if you push too much and blow up. And even if you make it to the end, the toll can be catastrophic.

How long are you running at redline? How are you refueling? Are you giving yourself some silence and rest or just picking up your phone to zone out for a bit and trick your mind into thinking you are resting? Are you running on empty? How hard are you pushing yourself? Are you just waiting for a crash or waiting to blow up?

How about you? Which activities in your life make you feel alive? Which activities make you tense and have a sense of anxiety or deep dread leading up to them? Why? What is it about you and those activities? What makes you smile? What makes you cry? What makes you *want* to jump out of bed in the morning? For me, it has become writing. I put my pen on the page, and it goes. So fun. So invigorating. I think how the reader will respond and try to guess which one of my life lessons might help someone else become their best version.

Which people are you pumped to get to see and which ones make you cringe? What is it about them? And as you meet new people, how you react when you see them or think about them will help you discern if they are someone that you might want in your inner circle, or equally important, they may be someone who will drag you down! And you don't need any part of that!

Unfortunately, sometimes, you need to take some body blows in life to figure these things out. Sometimes, you just need to try something new to see if you like it. And it is okay if you do not. Today, we went to a shooting range with my brother-in-law and his wife. I had no idea if Amy and Jace would enjoy it, but they had a blast. They tried something new and loved it.

This is your life. You get one chance. Give yourself permission to like and not like things. Even if your best friend or significant other or spouse lives and breathes golf, you do not have to. You may, however, need to show at least a little bit of interest so you can ask good questions and be interested. But please, oh please, don't live your life the way others expect you to live. That's not life. That's a script. To a movie that is really going to stink. Live your life! Figure out what makes you happy and something that pays the bills—if you are really lucky, they'll be the same thing.

There are people who say find something you love and you will never work a day in your life. That is great for them, but what if we aren't there? How bad do we feel about that? I am a dentist, and I love the relationships I have formed but I can't say I jump out of bed and can't wait to come to work every single day to work on teeth. But I do get very excited to spend the day with people. That is what I am about. And that is okay! It's your life. It's your journey. Say it with me, "It's my life!" I get one chance at it. I want to be my best self. Now say it again! Don't conform completely to other's expectations. Live your life. Live it to the full. Make other people's lives better along the way. That's living! That's really good living!

Knowing is half the battle—and maybe even much more. And self-awareness is knowing you, knowing a lot about you and then making life decisions based on how you feel. You do not need to keep playing golf if you don't like it, no matter how much someone else wants you to. You will resent it. You will become bitter. Those are bad things. You don't have to stay on your career path or in your job. You are not responsible for others' expectations or their happiness. This is your life.

Does watching the news cause you to get hyper and fired up? Turn it off for a while or a season. Does your friend's or spouse's or child's phone use drive you absolutely bonkers? Tell them. Work it out. Make it better. Have the tough conversation. Do you have an addictive personality? Do you go all in on whatever your new interest is? Know this about yourself. Tell your trusted advisors. Have them help keep tabs on you. Keep you accountable. More about this later.

Do you need accountability to read your Bible or to stay off your phone or not to text and drive or not to overeat or to exercise? Tell someone. Have them hold you accountable. There is power in having to come clean about your actions with someone you care about. Don't fight your battles alone or in secret. Get it out of the darkness and into the light! Strip it of its power! I am not sure if you know this, but things we hide and keep in the darkness hold power over us. Tell someone about it. The shame doesn't stick as well if we tell someone else and get it out in the open. Out in the light.

I feel like if we got our screen time published for all to see, I bet we would put our phone down more regularly. I am glad it isn't! I bet if everyone knew we had a few too many drinks or bought too many things online or bought too many baseball cards (this would be me!), we might not be so prone to those behaviors. I really don't want others to know my screen time or my shopping habits, but if it gets to be a problem, I need some accountability!

So spend some time in reflection. Alone. Think about you. This is not selfish in any way. This is not narcissistic. This will help you help others because self-awareness is a big key to becoming other-focused. Lack of self-awareness causes us to be self-protective, which can be very selfish. What makes you happy? What makes you sad? What gives you a sense of accomplishment? What takes up too much of your sixteen hours of discretionary time? Are there things (good or bad) that turn your sixteen hours into eighteen or twenty hours and kill your sleep? And are they good or bad things?

And what about oversleeping? This is something I am certainly not familiar with personally, but I am told this can be a sign of chronic depression. And chronic depression is certainly not lessening in the pandemic! You can have too much of a good thing. I am not talking about that miraculous ten hour night of sleep that your body really needed. I am talking about the every single night ten plus hour nights of sleep. It may be a sign that something is wrong. It may be your body's cry for help.

Just learn about you! And use what you learn to be honest with others. This self-awareness is good stuff, but you can't rush it. Make a list of ten things you have learned about yourself, and then consider sharing with one of your trusted advisors. And maybe hear their list as well. Here are a few of mine:

- I have an addictive personality. I must be careful when I start something new because I am all-in.
- I am highly relational. I do not love small talk. Let's really share life. I can talk weather or COVID-19 only so many times in a day before I implode. And I am a dentist. So you can imagine how many of these conversations I have.
- When I commit, I go all in, so I have to make sure I do not have too many commitments.
- I am more introverted than most people think I am, so I need some downtime to recharge. I cannot always be the life of the party, although I am a talker.
- I have to be careful to count the cost of a project or a challenge because I have went all in too many times only to find out that the end result was not worth the effort and sacrifice.
- I don't sit well or do well with time that is not programmed, but I am learning to love and embrace these times, as it is in those moments that spontaneity and rich experiences can be found. Sunday afternoons are absolutely amazing, by the way, if you have never noticed!
- I am constantly battled by the four horsemen of my apocalypse—fear, worry, stress, and anxiety.
- When I don't pray for extended periods of time, everything in my life is off. Prayer centers me. Brings me back to the middle.
- I love to hear people say nice things about me. I try to pour out for others. I love to get a little back. I like to know I made a difference.
- I am fiercely loyal. I got your back. Especially my family and my dental team. Don't mess with them. I won't tolerate it.

These are just a few of mine. Think of yours. It is a great and worthwhile exercise. Then run them by someone to see how well they know you or how well they feel you know yourself. Use some of these revelations to help live your best life and crush the false sense of urgency.

Other people like to share what they see about you. It's easy for someone to be an expert on someone else but not know themselves. It is easy to give advice without knowing the whole story of someone else. It takes time to develop self-awareness.

Journaling can really help. Grab a journal. Personally, I like the Moleskine journals. They have been my go to for more than ten years, and I have a big stack of the ones I have filled up over the years, and occasionally I go back and reread them as a sign of how life has changed and the lessons I have learned. If you haven't figured it out yet, I am a bit old school. I like pen and paper. You can use your phone or computer if you like but there is something pure to me about a notebook and a pen.

Here is a great book to read if you are interested in learning a method for journaling- The Bullet Journal Method: Track the Past, Order the Present, Design the Future by Ryder Carroll. Check it out if journaling interests you or you want to learn more about it.

Moleskine even makes smaller journals you can keep in your pocket or on your desk or your bedside table. Make notes in them, observations of your day, especially things like this:

> This thing happened and I feel _____, and I
> need _____.

Be honest. This is for your eyes. For example, today, I was asked to go to dinner with this friend. I was immediately excited and couldn't wait to finalize plans. Or today, John asked me to serve on a nonprofit board, and as he said it, I felt anxiety rising. Or today, I saw this person I used to work with. It reminded me that I am happy I don't work there anymore.

Keep a gratitude journal. At the end of the day, write down five things you are thankful for from that day. End your day with gratitude. Sounds like a good way to get ready to sleep! This is how I use the small journals.

Or last night I slept like schmaltz (translation = poorly) after staying up too late, and I felt I was behind the eight ball. Or when I got home from work a little late last week and my spouse really let me have it. I need her to extend me a little grace, but on the other hand, I need to communicate a little better with her when I am going to be late. And the reality is this- I am late for a variety of reasons. Sometimes my patients kept me there late. Sometimes my day was crazy and I needed fifteen minutes to zone out or decompress from the day before I come home. Maybe I looked at my email and flipped out as I saw what needed attention and chipped away a bit before heading home. The point is this- communicate. And know what you need.

Self-awareness is huge! As you develop it, you may become more equipped to know which situations bring you joy and which bring you stress, which relationships help you and which you need to keep at arm's length, what makes your head spin and what makes it be still. Definitely journal about these things, and try to incorporate the good into your life and watch out for the bad.

This life is a journey. Your journey! So give yourself some grace. Rome wasn't built in a day, and these patterns of urgency have been growing for years. Slow, intentional, deliberate, careful dismantling of the stronghold of the false sense of urgency is the key to lasting change. A quick fix will not work here and will ultimately send you in the wrong direction making things worse. And that is not what any of us needs. A quick fix would be some cheesy self-talk designed to distract your mind. It is like a band-aid. It covers up the problem and temporarily holds it together. You have to do the work. Lasting change will come if you get to the root of the problem.

We have all done this: we wake up one morning and say we are going to do better at this or that. We pledge to ourselves we will do better. Here is the line in the sand. And do we even make it to lunchtime? Past breakfast? Change takes time and work, but it is worth it!

Chapter 5

DON'T ALWAYS MEASURE YOUR DAY!

Stop measuring days by degree of productivity and start measuring them by degree of presence.

—*Alan Watts*

Some days will be very productive and others will not—at least by the normal metrics we use. And that is okay! Have you ever had a day that was just busywork, a day when you felt as if you did nothing other than return emails and clear your inbox? How about a day in which all you did was attend meetings? How about the day your to-do list grew and you crossed off nothing? As a dentist, my day can be full of short appointments that make me feel as if I didn't accomplish much of anything.

How do those days make you feel? How about if you are a stay-at-home mom and your entire list for the day was to clean the main floor of your house and you didn't get that done because your little workers and their constant need for your supervision? Or what if you did get the house in order and no one cares? No one appreciates your work? No one noticed. How do we feel if we get to the end of the day and have "nothing" to show for it? Are we stressed about that? Will we try to do better tomorrow? Do we feel like a failure? And if we do, does that feeling carry over into our other relationships as we have a pity party, or are we able to simply chalk it up to a day that didn't move the needle like we would have hoped?

My friend Kevin, as in the one from my inner circle, taught me the phrase "move the needle," and I love it. When reflecting on your day, you can consider whether or not you moved the needle. It is a good metric.

And what about the other type of days, when we do feel productive? You moved the needle. You checked off tasks. Your to-do list didn't stand a chance with your laser focus. You just felt flow, that feeling that the day is rolling along all day. But as you reflect on the day, what might you have missed? Were you so focused on your list or on your agenda that you missed a chance to have a conversation with a coworker who was really in need of a touchpoint or a talk? Were you so focused that you missed chances to build relationships or encourage someone else?

A day is a funny thing to use as a measuring stick. We all

have twenty-four hours, as we discussed (well, really sixteen). Sometimes those hours go by fast. Sometimes they go by slowly, at a snail's pace. Sometimes we are having lunch and we feel like we have already accomplished enough for two days. Sometimes we hit the end of the day and we don't even feel as if we ever got fully started on the tasks at hand. And we have to sit in that.

So here it is again—we are on a journey! And it is dangerous to put too much pressure on one snippet of the journey, on one snapshot. There are 365 of these days in a single year! We are on a journey. What is the cumulative effect of the journey? Overall, are you moving the needle in the right direction? Are the things that cause you to think you had a really unproductive day really so bad? Did you really waste most of the day on social media (probably bad), or were you available for someone else and did you help them navigate their journey and become a better version of themselves?

Be really careful how you measure a day. Think about it for a bit. If it is really productive, you may be super excited! But you may also be thinking, *Meh, I needed it to be that way, and it was.* You expected it, and it fulfilled your expectation. Hardly a cause for celebration. Or it ended up not being productive, and you were bummed and beat yourself up about it. What is worse? Your opinion that you did not get much accomplished or the shame and condemnation that you put yourself through over it?

Don't beat yourself up about it. Reflect on your day and move on. There's another one coming tomorrow! In all metrics of life and the ways you measure yourself, if *meh* is the best measurement you can get, then ditch the metric. Try something else, another way to measure.

In my profession, it is easy to measure a day based on production—how many procedures were accomplished, especially the ones with a higher monetary value. How much did my team accomplish today in terms of the bottom line, both through what we produced and through what we collected in terms of patient payments? This is what the majority of the practice-management consultants teach us. Production and collections. Then do it again tomorrow. Measure everything.

But to me, that kind of thinking is not sustainable as the only way to measure a day, a week, a month, or even a year. Sometimes, more productive appointments are set up by less productive appointments. And even more importantly, if all my happiness and joy is based on those daily numbers, I am certainly set up for failure. There has to be more to all of this than how we did today on procedures!

Sometimes in life, we simply have to realize that what we have been doing simply isn't working. It's time for something new—a new wineskin, if you will. If you have new wine or a new skill, you need a new wineskin or a new vessel to hold it. The old wineskin can't hold the new wine. It has already been stretched to its limit from the old wine or old skill that was in it. It will bust at the seams with new wine. It isn't ready for a new skill. And you need a change in you to handle this new paradigm. The old just won't cut it.

What about this for a possibility? Instead of putting such a heavy load of pressure on ourselves for each individual day, each individual meeting, each individual project, maybe we could look at each day, each meeting, each project, and each task as part of our journey, as part of our process of becoming who we are and who we are meant to be.

Then, at the end of the week, reflect on the week as a whole— what went well, what didn't go so well or as planned. What can we do better on? But also, what *did* we do well on? We must give ourselves some grace. There are certainly things we did well even if the week as a whole was a disappointment.

We need to find a way to take some of the pressure off ourselves. We put so much pressure on what we need to get done today that we often leave no room for what might happen or what could happen. Then, at the end of the day or the end of the week, take some time and consider how you did. But do not allow any shame or condemnation. And as my dad has famously said, "Never *should* on yourself." It's really great advice. Don't dwell on what you did wrong or what you should have done, but instead, plot a course to do better.

If you are unhappy, do not simply wallow in your unhappiness. Consider how you can improve. How could tomorrow or next week be better? Or maybe, if you think about it, today was actually pretty good *but*. Maybe I just put expectations on myself that were too high, and in doing so, I set myself up for failure.

Look at each day through a fair lens. Please do not put expectations on a day that simply cannot be met no matter how spectacular the day is or how much you rocked it. Where's the hope for a win in that? What happens if you wake up and your mind is racing and you think, *Okay, today this and this, and this must happen, and they must happen this way for me to have a good day*? All right, but what if those things don't happen? Or what happens if the stars align and all those things happen? Well, you expected them to, so there is really no excitement when there should be a load of excitement. You got it all done! The stars aligned! You rocked it out! But no, you expected all of it, so there is that recurring feeling of *meh*. Of being melancholy about it.

Try to set realistic expectations for a day, and leave a little room to be wowed if the day progresses better than you expected. Isn't it so much more enjoyable if you get to the end of the day and you are pleasantly surprised instead of *Ho hum* or *Meh, I guessed it would be like that, and it was*?

I want to introduce a concept that my pastor and friend, Kevin Korver, has shared with our church. And it is a beautiful and significant concept. Living in expectancy vs. expectation. Expectation is the waking up with a spinning head and a task list running circles in your mind, and I have to nail it and all these things for it to be a good day. Expectancy is more of a what might happen today in the small margins or meetings if I am present and allow it to happen. Who might I get to interact with or share a smile with? In which life could I get a chance to make a difference by being present? Because when you live with expectation, you tend to be laser focused, with no room for what might happen. If it doesn't serve the tasks, it isn't worth it.

Expectancy is a great way to live. But please hear what it is not. I am not suggesting a la-di-da way of life, where you casually move from thing to thing with no seeming order. Believe me. I know schedules. For eighteen years, I have been owned by the fifteen-minute increment of time. And before that, seven years of college. And before that, the schedules of school. You get it. My point is that we need schedules, but we also need some margin for what might happen. All I am suggesting is to try to wake up thinking about what might happen today in those times that are available in the margins if we are available and not simply running ourselves into the ground.

There will be days of expectation and deadlines and running yourself into the ground. That is life, but that cannot be every day. We weren't built for that. There will be a crash, either physical, emotional, mental, or some other way, but it is coming. Red-line driving is not sustainable. And red-line working is also not sustainable.

And while we are on the subject of margin, do you have any? And do you know what margin is? Margin is the little bits of time in between other things that we can use to briefly recharge our brain—exercise or going for a walk or having a conversation with someone or just sitting in silence. I am here to tell you that you need some. It really is nonnegotiable if you are to live your life to your full potential, to be your best version, your best self.

Lack of margin tells your spouse or friend or child that you can't talk with them now but will try to find a time, which you know you won't. It tells your kids you are too busy to play with them, and so eventually, after hearing this so much, they stop asking. It tells friends you can't get coffee or dinner or talk with them because you are busy. Oh, you know, life is just so busy right now. We say it all the time, almost like a badge of honor. How are you? Busy. Real busy. I started hearing that more and more in August of 2020 and it continues to ramp up as the pandemic eases it's grip on life as we know it in 2021. Life seemed to slow to a halt in mid-March through at least May or June, but how quickly we have gone right back to busy, busy, busy. It makes me sad. We need some margin to be able to drop what we are doing in favor of something that might be better. There are different seasons of life. Sometimes, you will have very little margin and sometimes more, but you need *some*.

When I did triathlon, I was all consumed. I missed so many chances to do life with my family, with my kids, with friends because I had to train. My twenty-plus hours of training each week ruthlessly devoured any margin I hoped to have. I was a robot. Over the course of a calendar year, I missed two workouts. Two. Out of 500 plus. That's how robotic I had become.

And now, I don't have triathlon, but I tend to waste my time on my phone or random "perceived urgencies" that pop up but really suck away any margin time I have had. So what are your time sucks or time sinks? What are the things that are robbing your margin? Is there a better way? How can you be more available?

In all of this, please remember this phrase: *no judgment, just journey.* You may need to put it on a Post-it note in places you regularly look. It is a powerful reminder. I know I already sound like a broken record, but you are on a journey. A day does not define you. Okay, it may have been a really huge day, I understand, but it is part of your journey, so don't judge yourself for how this day or this week or this meeting or this project went. Don't judge others. That is just poor form. Help others instead of judging them.

Consider once again, everything that happens in your life is part of your journey. If you are constantly critiquing your life and being hard on yourself and being your worst critic, you will have a rough journey, but if you reflect on your days and try to start them with expectancy, slowly or maybe even quickly, you will become a better version of yourself, a more gracious version of yourself. People will see a difference. You will not be so critical. You will not be so cynical. You will maybe even start to seem optimistic. Think about a life in which you don't put so much pressure on yourself. That sounds pretty epic to me.

In closing this chapter, I'll say a day is simply that—a day. God willing, we will have more days. So don't put expectations on a day that cannot possibly be met. Reflect on your days. What went well? What didn't go well? And why? What could you do better next time? And if you can't see what you could have done better, seek wise counsel as to what went wrong. Then be gracious to yourself. You can be your best friend or your worst enemy based on how you treat yourself and your self-talk.

We only get one chance at this life, so let's not spend it tearing ourselves and others down. Instead, could we try to make our own corner of the world a little better each moment. Each day.

No judgment, just journey.

Chapter 6

THE ADDICTIVE PERSONALITY

My problem is I'm an addictive personality. I can't have one coffee. I can't eat one piece of chocolate.

—*Guy Pearce*

This chapter may or may not strike a chord with you individually. If it does or does not, that's okay, but please keep reading. However, chances are that if this doesn't ring true for you personally, you know someone or a few someone's for whom this is absolutely true. I am talking about the addictive personality.

My mentor from several years ago, John, introduced this term to me while we were having one of our many meetings in the basement of my dental office. I remember it so clearly as John was seated in an oversized comfortable chair and I was eating my lunch on the couch. The sun was shining in the windows. This was one of those bookmark moments in life, one you tend to remember very explicitly.

Let me just say that John is an exemplary human being. He has incredible wisdom and is a great listener, great attributes for a mentor. He has a body that is badly broken down, but his spirit and his faith are strong. He would have every right to be cynical in life, but he has chosen not to be. I admire that about John.

The first question John asked me on the first day we got together cut directly to my identity: "Who is Eric Recker without all the races, without all the awards, without all the initials after his name, without all of the accolades?" Whoa, buddy. Slow down the train. Let's maybe ease into this thing a little bit. Maybe even a little chitchat (although you know how I feel about that). But no, he cut right to the chase, and I am forever thankful to him that he was willing to go there right off the bat.

Throughout my life, with a history of being bullied for the better part of six years in what I would consider to be formative years, I have overcompensated by trying to define myself by accomplishment. You don't want this fourth-grader to be on either kickball team? Okay, I will become a robot and dominate at everything so people will have to pick me. (How's that for self-awareness). And so I did. And I could list a whole bunch of accomplishments or show you a few cardboard boxes full of medals and ribbons and trophies. I could show you initials I have added to my professional name. I could show you big numbers when it comes to my continuing education hours. I could show you many things. But it all led to one thing, according to John.

I have an addictive personality, and it just feeds the false sense of urgency, like a synchronized swimming exhibition. They go hand in hand. Have you ever watched synchronized swimming? I will admit, I don't love it by any means, but I am impressed by the work and coordination it takes to get to that place of performance and competition. The addictive personality feeds the false sense of urgency and vice versa, like a well-choreographed dance. They go hand in hand.

There's a really a simple test to see if you or someone you know is affected by the addictive personality "disorder." When you start something, do you sort of try it out and see how it goes, or are you all ready to buy the gear and jump in with both feet? Will you finish what you started at all costs, or can you walk away? Will you spend time, energy, and resources (often including those you really cannot afford to spend) to feed your new thing?

For me, it has been school work, getting into dental school, trying to be the best in my class, getting the most continuing-education hours, triathlon, collecting baseball cards and baseball photos, bike racing, buying new bikes, buying the perfect Jeep, getting my Fellowship in the Academy of General Dentistry, (FAGD) and getting my pilot's license. Then there was my Mastership, (MAGD), and now I'm working on my lifelong service recognition (LLSR, it's really all about acronyms!). It is always something with me. All these things I have started, I have seen through to completion—some at great cost financially, relationally, and in terms of time spent.

My wife gives me the stink eye when I mention trying something new. She is completely supportive of me, and for that, I am forever thankful. I know she is supportive, because if she weren't, she would have been long gone by now! I can be a lot, but she knows. If I tell her I am thinking about riding my bike across my home state of Iowa in a day, she knows to plan on it happening. She knows if I start discussing a new vehicle or bike, then we better get ready because it is going to happen. And if I say I might try to do a 7-mile open-water swim with a bunch of buddies, mark the calendar.

I can only imagine what Amy thought when I started talking about writing a book. I can only imagine what her mind was telling her when I mentioned the possibility of speaking and writing and coaching and consulting. What can I say? I married a very supportive woman. For that, among so many other things, I am blessed. I am so thankful for the fabulous Amy Recker.

I just have it. I can literally spend hours scouring auctions and sending emails and looking online and looking at message boards looking for the perfect baseball card or photo. I can waste so much time and—let's be honest—spend so much money on these things. But then I get to the inevitable point that most people with addictive personalities get to: the end didn't justify the means. All those hours training. All those hours searching online. All those mornings away from home. And then the end result of all of that effort and striving is a big question: Was it worth it? Did the end result justify all the energy, time, money, effort?

I am a thrill-of-the-hunt kind of guy. I research. I plan. I scheme. I make these lists of auctions that I am tracking on legal pads. Yes, as I said before, I am old-school. I like pen (or pencil) and paper! I relentlessly track the minimum bid, the current bid, how many bidders and watchers are participating, and then decide which, if any, I will chase. And then, if I win, how many times has the package come from the auction house, and I open it, and meh. It is still a really cool piece and often a great addition to my collection, but it let me down. It wasn't what I hoped it would be.

I finally hit this realization and the self-awareness that goes along with it on the top of Mount Princeton, near Leadville,

Colorado, in August 2017. My schedule for the week was simple but busy.

Tuesday: drive a rental RV from Omaha, Nebraska, to Leadville, Colorado, with my son and father-in-law and brothers-in-law, about a thirteen-hour drive with stops.

Wednesday: up early with the sun to hike Mount Princeton, a 14er. A 14er is a mountain with an elevation greater than 14,000 feet. Colorado is awesome for many reasons and one of them is having 53 such peaks. Some ambitious climbers try to conquer all of them. This climb after a day of travel from low altitude is a pretty lofty goal as a flatlander. Iowa, where I left twenty-four hours earlier, is less than 1,000 feet of elevation.

Thursday: whitewater rafting. And fairly aggressive. What I hadn't counted on is the fact you basically squat on the side of the raft for the duration of the trip. Bad idea 2 days before a long bike race.

Friday: race briefing for the Leadville 100 MTB and then some Jeep off-roading.

Saturday: 100 miles of mountain bike racing all above 9,000 feet with the top elevation being 12,600 feet.

On top of Mount Princeton on Wednesday, I had the crystal-clear realization that finishing the bike race on Saturday would not give me the high that I was seeking. It would not be worth the more than twelve hours of biking I had been doing each week for the previous eight months. It would not be worth the Friday or Saturday weekly seven-hour bike rides on gravel roads. Have you ever had that thought that what you are chasing so hard after might not be worth the chase? Long story short, it wasn't. I crossed the finish line, and it was hollow. I collected my award the next day, a big belt buckle, along with my finisher sweatshirt, and we drove home. And I was cured of endurance racing. Four years later, I am still cured. Still in remission, so to speak. I have no desire to go through all that again. Don't get me wrong, it was a wonderful guys trip. But the trophy was lackluster.

However, I still struggle with the addictive personality. It has just been redirected. While my dental office was closed due to COVID-19, I endured almost a hundred hours of continuing-education videos trying to learn whatever I could about the virus and about new procedures and about reopening, and I probably also spent another hundred hours on my reopening plan, as I had to basically trash it and start over again, countless times. Then, when it was time to open back up, I spent countless hours stressing about it.

My point in all this is this: the addictive personality is a fickle mistress. It is never satisfied. It is always demanding more, always needing to be fed, to be stoked. I was reminded of it very powerfully by the 2017 movie *The Greatest Showman*. I am not typically a musical kind of guy, but that is one great movie. And the song "Never Enough" gets me every time:

> All the stars from a thousand spotlights, all the stars we steal from the night sky will never be enough, never be enough. Towers of gold are still too little these hands could hold the world but it'll never be enough. Never be enough.

I have seen this to be true. It is impossible to satisfy the addictive personality, and the addictive personality feeds the false sense of urgency so well. Triathlon training: *I need to train. I need to eat well. I need to get my nasty, sweaty clothes cleaned so I can have them to train more. I need to change my bike tires or my tubes.*

And watch out for the night before a race or the morning of a race. I am a stressed-out mess. It was never worth all that. I literally didn't sleep the night before a race, ever. More nights than not, I would lie awake the entire night. All that for the right to pay an entry fee and receive what ends up being a very expensive medal.

Or in the case of auctions: *This auction is closing at this time on eBay. This auction ends this time in the night.*

For continuing education: *This test to get my AGD fellowship needs me to study this much.*

It is literally always something.

So you are thinking at this point, *Okay, Eric. We get it. You have showed us what this is all about and how it has affected you. So what do we do about it? How does never enough become enough?*

Well, as I have said before in the book, self-awareness is huge in this life. GI Joe says knowing is half the battle, and in this case, it may be even more than half. If you are deciding at this point that you have an addictive personality, or if you are one of us who is "all-in and at all costs," then own it. It is what it is. It is part of your journey. It is part of the fabric of who you are. *And it is okay.* And part of it may be why you have been successful in life.

Please spend a grand total of zero minutes judging and condemning yourself about it. Seriously. Don't just say you can change or drop it. However old you are, you have grown into this attribute for that many years. I have more than thirty-five years of experience growing into it. I believe that for me, it started when I was seven or eight years old.

Own it. Recognize it. Deal with it. It is also part of who you are. And quite frankly, it is probably part of why you are good at what you do! Think about it. The addictive personality also creates drive and causes you to push yourself, which, when harnessed in a correct and healthy manner, can really be a good thing!

But definitely recognize it. It is okay. Just realize that when you see something you might like to get involved with, take the time to count the cost first. How all-in might you become with this new thing? This new adventure. This new venture. This new hobby. How much time might be required? What sacrifices will you need to make to see this thing through? Because you know you and how you will see it through. What sacrifices will your family need to make for you to see this through or get involved?

Is your family willing to make those sacrifices? Is your family able to make those sacrifices? Have you had a family meeting to discuss this? Things that are new and shiny and exciting often lose their luster when you look carefully at what is needed to see this through to the end.

Think of it this way: If you wanted to do an Ironman triathlon, would you rather find out that it wasn't going to work for your family before you started training, buying a bike and a wetsuit and running shoes and bike shorts and a helmet and triathlon jerseys and a Garmin watch and so many other things? Or would you rather find out twenty weeks in, after you have bought all this stuff and paid the race fee (which, by the way, is a load of cash) and are fully committed?

If you want to start a new job, would you like to find out before you start that the commute and hours will crush your soul, steal your margin, and ruin any semblance of family time you had? Or would you like to wait until you have quit your job with nothing to fall back on to find out the strain of this new opportunity?

If you want to take up golf, are you able and willing to give up six to eight hours on a weekend day to get in the perfect eighteen holes? Buy the gear, the shoes, the membership, the cart rental? Or is that something that might be better if someone else in your family was interested?

Hunting is huge around Iowa, where I live. As I write this in early fall, hunting season is upon us, and there are a whole lot of people who participate. If you are a hunter or are considering becoming one, I also have to ask if your family is willing not to see you during shotgun or bow-hunting season for deer or whatever you like to hunt. Not to mention purchasing the guns and ammo and gear and tags and travel expenses and guides.

You have to slow down. You have to count the cost. You have to take the time and analyze as best as you can and make a rational decision. Your addictive personality is always hungry or maybe even hangry. Hangry means super hungry! I have also been told it means hungry plus angry. Either way, it is significant! It is always looking for parts of your soul to devour. It wants to be fed. But you are still in the driver's seat, and you get to decide if you feed it or let it starve a bit. That is all on you.

Not all that is shiny and new is worthy of your attention. It is not all worthy of your time. And anything you give your time to, that time has to come from somewhere. And at best, you have sixteen hours in a day. Is it worth it?

And just as an aside, these things I have mentioned are not bad things, per se. Anything can be bad if it takes too much of your time and destroys your primary relationships and zaps your margin. All I am asking is that you count the cost. And try to find things you might be able to do with your family and friends.

Activities always seem to work better in family systems if multiple family members participate. For example, when I fly, the boys often go with me, and Jace has even started taking flying lessons. It's a winning formula if you can find activities that you and your family love.

Last but not least: one other antidote to the addictive personality is contentment. This is not a popular word. The American dream was not built on contentment. The American and world economic engine is not based on contentment. Most marketing is anti-contentment. You need this. *Life would be better if only ...*

The search for contentment is tough, but if you can look at what you have and what you can do with what you have, then maybe you might not need to feed the addictive personality. Take some time to look around you. See what's there. See who is there. There might be some pretty good options right next to you.

And if you want to try something new out to see how it feels, and if you might like it, rent the bike. Borrow some clubs and take a few lessons. Take a hunter's safety course and talk to some buddies about it. Take the drive for the new commute. Can you tolerate it? The more we commit to something new, the more we feel we need to see it through. Take a test drive. See how it fits you and those who matter to you. New and shiny doesn't always equal lasting, fulfilling, and life-giving.

Chapter 7

BE PRESENT

Wherever you are, be all there.

—*Jim Elliot*

F unny story. Long before I decided to write this book, I determined that my word for the year would be *presence*. Each year, I try to pick a word to center myself around for that year. This year, it is *presence*, with one major goal: wherever I am, I am fully there. Not one foot in the room and one out. Not checking other things on my phone while talking to someone. Just being there. One hundred percent. Full attention. Full listening. Full eye contact. Full and complete focus.

A quick surface skim here on picking your word for the year (which, by the way, you absolutely should do). Check out the book *One Word That Will Change Your Life*, co-authored by Jon Gordon. Jon Gordon just happens to be one of the most perpetually positive people I have met, and he is bent on making sure positivity catches on even in the hardest of times.

One word for the year is a rallying cry. A thermometer. A barometer. An anchor. A reminder of what you are hoping for in the upcoming or present year. I usually start contemplating my word for the next year around Thanksgiving time to give it some time to marinate on it and decide which word suits me best. I like Thanksgiving time because it is typically when we are more in an attitude of gratitude and it is easier for us to be forward-thinking and ponder how we might be just as thankful or more next year at this time. It is a great reflection time. Your word can be any number of words, but it has to be your word, not someone else's. You have to do the work to discover it, but it isn't difficult, and the rewards and potential are great!

After you have chosen a word, share it with your friends and family and your inner circle, and hopefully they'll share theirs as well. If they don't have one, you can introduce the concept and encourage them to find theirs as well. It can be perfect for accountability, so take the time to do this very important step. I don't care what time of year you decided to read this book. As long as it isn't late in the evening on December 31, there is time for a word for this year! And if it happens to be late in the evening on December 31, guess what: you have next year's word!

Just be sure and count the cost of your word. You need a word that you will want to see regularly and aspire toward. Then put it on Post-it notes around your home or office or in your car. Set alarms on your phone to remind you of it. And then live it!

Onto presence. I own a dental office, a busy one. There are two to three dentists and usually five to six hygienists working, as well as assistants and my administrative team. So needless to say, I have a lot going on and a lot going through my mind. I suspect it will be this way until my name is not the top one on the sign. Add into this equation a mind that has highly embraced the false sense of urgency for most of my life, and you have a perfect recipe for distraction.

I am famous for being physically in one space and mentally in another. I am famous for trying to have a conversation while doing something else on my phone. Here's the thing: you cannot multitask, and secretly, I think you know it. The secret's up about multitasking, and the newer studies show it. Some people can slide seemingly effortlessly from one task to another, but their energy cannot be split among multiple tasks. If you really are trying to do multiple things all at the same time, you will probably just be lousy at all of them. Sorry for my language and my bluntness, but you know this is true.

You cannot be in one place mentally and another physically. The results are catastrophic, and what suffers in all of this, the most important thing, is relationships. If someone is trying to have a conversation with you and you whip out your phone to check something or answer a text, you could have just as easily flipped the other person off, as that is what your actions are saying to them. What they have to say is just not as important as whatever you wanted to look at on your phone.

Wherever you are, be there. Be fully there, not thinking about the previous thing or meeting or conversation, not thinking about the next thing. Just be there. You may have something really big coming up, but is it worth forsaking what is right in front of you? And remember this: your big thing may be coming up, but for the person you are interacting with, right now, very well might be *their* big thing! Or your attentiveness and presence may make all the difference to them.

If staying at work ten extra minutes helps you be fully present for dinner at home instead of thinking about that thing you didn't get done at the office, stay the extra ten minutes. You may not be able to do this every time, but your family will appreciate your full presence at the dinner table! And yes, if at all possible, you should have dinner with them at the dinner table.

The bottom line is this: set yourself up so you can get your stuff done and free your mind so you can spend good quality time with the person or people right in front of you. If you can't do this or you feel you are unable to be fully present, might I humbly suggest you might not be in the right vocation or job. Consider this. There will always be an excuse for why not to be fully present, but if you always use this excuse, you might need a career pivot or a job change.

It isn't fair to you or those around you to get only a part of you. And it can't be fun to always have your head in multiple places. Believe me, I know about that one. Working on one patient, and three hygienists are waiting as patiently as they can be for me to come check their patients and my next patient is in the waiting room and my front desk team member has three questions she needs to ask me. All those things are important, but it is challenging to give each of them my undivided attention.

How about trying this out: wherever you are, let those people know they are your first priority by your actions toward them. Listen. Truly listen. Don't just wait to talk. Engage them. Ask good questions so they can share more. We have all been around the person who just wants to constantly talk. It is kind of exhausting. You can almost see their wheels turning waiting, or you to stop talking so they can. You know they have comprehended nothing of what you have just said. They are not listening to anything you said, and if you don't stop talking soon enough for them, they will just cut you off and dive right in themselves.

How does it make you feel when someone treats you in that manner? They don't pay attention to you. They check their phone constantly. They are obviously somewhere else mentally. And then there are those who can't wait to talk and also like to embellish a little so their story can be a bit better, a bit more sensational than yours. Don't be that person. You don't want to be around them, so do yourself a favor and don't be them!

Others deserve your best, and that includes your presence. For me at work, if one of my team wants my undivided attention, it has to be a one-on-one conversation in my personal office, with no distractions. When someone wants to talk with me, I assume it is going to be significant, and we create space for it. I am very protective of my schedule, so it has to be in a space that is available, but I am happy to talk with them at the appropriate time and see what we can figure out. The difficulty comes when someone wants to talk at the end of the morning and I have a meeting already scheduled for lunch and I physically have no time. But we find a way to make it work, and I always try to have the conversation same day so we can address it right away.

Wherever you are, simply be there. Show up with a clear mind as much as possible. Keep your phone in your pocket, and *if* you need to check it (which, let's be honest, you probably don't need to), then excuse yourself during an appropriate lull in the conversation. Check only what you need to check, and then get back to the conversation. Always count the cost and ask yourself, "Is what's on my phone more important than what's right in front of me?"

Be the kind of person you want to be around. I am guessing your favorite people are those who are good at presence. Be the kind of person you want to be friends with. That's a good start.

If you want to thrive, presence is nonnegotiable. You have to be present. You have to communicate. The false sense of urgency says you have all these other things to do, but do you? Really, do you? Are these other things really that important? Is a training session more important than time with your wife to catch up and share life and discuss some important life events? Is online shopping for who-knows what more important than a chance to catch up with a friend for coffee or a Facetime or Zoom meeting?

Please hear my where my heart is in saying this next part. My heart wants you to be your best version. Some of you may be offended by this next part, but that is not my intent. So please, grant me a huge umbrella of mercy, as my pastor says when he is about to say something that might ruffle some feathers.

Is being a mom 24/7 and not allowing a babysitter to watch your kids more important than a much-needed date night with your spouse? Dating your spouse is ridiculously important, by the way, because this is the person who will still be there after the kids go off to school, and you better work on that marriage, or you will be staring at a person you don't know and probably don't like someday before you know it. Do you really need to go into the office early every single day so that you miss breakfast with your family and are an absentee parent as your kids grow up right before your eyes?

These are tough decisions. A tough decision is anything that has good decisions on either side of it (or possibly bad on either side). You have had and will have countless tough decisions in your life. Good decisions, generally, in my humble opinion, involve relationships. Poor decisions, generally, involve solitary time or screen time alone. I will let you use your imagination there.

And what about as a leader? How much will your people respect you if they get your best? If they think and know you are really listening to them? Great leaders get the most out of their team, and it starts with being present and attentive. I don't know any way around it.

So here is my challenge for you: be present. This is another way you can do battle with the false sense of urgency. The more you are present and focused, the less you are drawn elsewhere, the less you have a desire to be elsewhere. And that is better for everyone. And I have a sneaking suspicion that you might just like the results.

Chapter 8

PHONES

Anybody have plans to stare at their phone
somewhere exciting this weekend?

—*Nitya Prakash*

Smartphone is definitely smarter than us
to be able to keep us addicted to it.

—*Munia Khan*

Oh, the phone. Where so I start? Oh wait, I already did start. The phone may be one of the worst contributors to the false sense of urgency! The false sense of urgency certainly existed before the phone, but with the help of the phone, it got on steroids and got bigger, more menacing, and occasionally more rage filled. The false sense of urgency demands allegiance as it nags and nags and nags at you until you slay it or give in. And most of the time, let's face it, we give in. It's easier. It's what we do.

How is there more of a false sense of urgency than a vibration here, a chime there, a ring tone, the familiar sound of a snap. Let's be honest here. Using one platform as an example, Snapchat is brilliant but horrible for people who struggle with the false sense of urgency, the need for instant gratification in picking up the phone and seeing what it is and the need to respond instantly. They have it figured out. Seriously, not good! It consumes the minds of so many. I have two boys at my house falling prey. I watch them as we are hanging out, and there is a different type of vibration, a different type of notification, and then they grab their phone and make some weird face or point their phone away and take a picture to send back, and that is it. All about streaks, I am told. Gotta keep up the streaks. Just consider how this stokes someone's urgency. Can't let my streaks end! Who haven't I replied to? Trying to keep it all up is tiring to me. But they seem to love it. But even if we go to a place where we don't have service, they have someone else do their streaks for them. Seriously. Urgency much?

Apple watches or any kind of smart watch, while allowing us to stay connected without our phones directly in our sight, make it easier to feed urgency, as now everything is right on your wrist. You don't even need to get your phone out to check the notification. And the more apps you have and the more notifications you set up, the more you can be bothered, interrupted, and distracted.

And, consequently, the more you can get distracted from being fully present, and the more your false sense of urgency helps encourage a shopping compulsion or addiction—you are one notification away from a new auction popping, a new sale, or a reminder of limited quantities—the greater the need to act now! Drop everything!

Phones are like the Lotus Casino cookies in the Percy Jackson novel *The Lightning Thief*. You try it, and the next thing you know, it is three hours later and you have gotten nothing done and your head is spinning and you are distracted and agitated. And quite honestly, you are a little detached from reality from a mind-numbing zone-out for three hours on your phone. It is so true. You know it has happened to you. Phones are time sucks. They are time sinks. And believe me, they are for me, as well. So please do not for one second read any of this as accusatory, because the first accusation would be right back at me!

We have a supercomputer at our fingertips, and while there are many advantages to that, technology comes with a price. The family out for dinner, all zoned out on their phones. The family car trip with Dad or Mom driving and everyone else in La La Land. Even our kids get digital babysitters these days. And the kids are lost in the maze just as much as adults are. And let's not even get into the issues of Internet porn and the dark web and other ways to get lost.

In 2020 and well into 2021 as I write, we had the Zoom meeting, where almost everyone was on their phone paying zero attention. And being stuck at home to work, I can imagine, is not helping with phone addictions.

Phones can be great, and they can be terrible. Social media, through its countless algorithms and advertising, has been designed to get you never to leave that platform. Not to be repetitive, but in order to further make the point- It's like the "Hotel California," the famous song by the Eagles: "You can check out any time you like, but you can never leave." I realize that is repetitive, but it is worth repeating. Refresh the feed, and there is more. Start reading comments, and you may never leave. And how bad are most of the comments? Are we even teaching spelling and grammar anymore?

And I think one of the most dangerous parts of all of this—or maybe *the* most dangerous part—is comparison culture, especially on Facebook. But as my fifteen-year-old readily told me, Twitter, Instagram, Snapchat, and TikTok are no different. It is an epidemic.

You can have the entire ideal Facebook life, or at least you are fooled into believing it. A quick scroll through your feed, and you are led to believe you can or should have this person's house or a nicer one, with this person's pool, complete with all the friends hanging around and partying, and this person's game room. And then you can have this one dude's sweet and caring wife with the body of this other guy's wife. And you can have her athletic kids with all the tournaments and medals with the brains and accomplishments of his kids and even get an honor roll sticker for your van or her sweet SUV. Then sprinkle in someone else's Jeep or convertible or SUV and someone else's vacation or adventures. Hey, why not? This woman's husband is a great chef, so let's have that as well. And that person's job looks better than mine, so I want that as well!

Is your head spinning yet? Academically, we know all this is not possible, but our hearts can be deceptive, and they can breed discontentment. What does discontentment do, and why is it dangerous? It feeds the false sense of urgency because all that is missing here is more money, right? So I just need to work harder or pick up an extra job or get some more money and get some more stuff, and then we will be good.

But we find ourselves working hard toward an unattainable goal, and the funny thing about unattainable goals is they are just that, but still we chase and feed the false sense of urgency, and we get super frustrated. Let's say we get the boat we always wanted and then it does what boats do: breaks down. And then what are we left with? Sink more money (that we probably don't have) into it, even though it is nowhere near paid off. And then we realize it will never become what we had hoped it would be. It is hollow. It was the thrill of the chase and an attempt at easy street, but sadly, easy street is paved with loads and loads of debt.

It is sort of like owning a pool- which I used to own. There's a funny expression about pools that I believe also applies to boats- the two best days with a pool- the day you open it for the first time and the day you fill it in. The same can be said of a boat. The day of purchase and the day of sale.

Be careful how much you envy someone else's anything, because you don't know the whole story or even the rest of the story. But as someone who often gets to hear the rest of the story through relationships and really getting to know people, the grass, almost invariably, is not as green on the other side as it appears. It is ridden with weeds and is much more high-maintenance than you had hoped for.

The athletic kid is on drugs. The honor-roll student is contemplating suicide. The house is mortgaged to the hilt. All of one's friends are only using them for the pool or game room or boat. The car or SUV or Jeep will probably never get fully paid off before it is repossessed. The other guy's wife is involved in a pyramid scheme. And the chef, well, let's just say, you don't even want to know. All people have bad stuff. We just don't show the stuff to others. The grass probably isn't greener. And even if it is, it isn't your grass!

So all of this to say, the phone is a vehicle to so many great things, but in addition to those great things, we have invented the greatest time sink known to man. Talking around the dinner table has been replaced by being engrossed in videos or social media. Shutting down at the end of the day and letting your brain relax has been replaced by lying in bed looking at our phones and wasting time and cutting into our sleep. We put things in our minds when they are trying to shut down; this is anything but conducive to sleep.

Some extra time in line at the grocery store or waiting for a fitting room in a store or when there is a red light or really any pause in life. Any lull in a conversation or even the slightest hint of an awkward silence, the phones are right out. We are so addicted. We can't keep them out of our hands!

If we continue to give our phones permission to breed discontentment and keep us locked in their algorithms, we lose. And we lose big. Our anxiety is up. Our fear is up. Our joy is absent. Our happiness is totally gone. But hey, we are connected! But are we? Are a few typed messages here or there really connection? What is the end game of all of this? What are we hoping for?

I know there are a lot of questions, but I truly think we need to keep our phone time in check if we want to have any hope of defeating the false sense of urgency. I guess we could come right out now and say it at this point: if you enjoy feeling a low-grade urgent anxiety about nothing all the time, then keep your phone constantly in your hand. Feed it. Stoke it. Obey its urges. Keep looking. Keep scrolling. Eat the Lotus Casino cookie. Get to the end of the day and realize that you truly did nothing. And that's okay, as not every day has to be super-productive. But in the course of doing nothing, which could have actually been relaxing, you got no rest. No respite. You just wasted time and probably money. If that is what you want, keep it up. But also remember, when it comes to wasting time, we only have about sixteen hours per day to choose what we do.

But there is a better way! Again, I will say this comes back to self-awareness. We need to know and realize and observe what our phones do to us (or, more appropriately, what we *let them* do to us). So let me offer a suggestion, if I may.

The Screen-Time Reduction Challenge

If you have an iPhone, it is super easy to check your screen time. You can get a weekly screen time report that actually breaks down your time into social networking, education, and other.

You can even see your top apps that contribute to screen time—or, better translated, the areas that suck most of your time. I am even assured by my friends who use Android phones that there are ways to track screen time on those devices. RescueTime is a pay app that allows you to do this.

There are two ways you can handle this challenge and there are actually variations and permutations on each. So get creative. Find out the best way to motivate yourself.

The first is the *group challenge*. The group can be any group you want it to be—family or friends or coworkers or neighbors. The idea is pretty simple. Everyone writes down their screen time average per week for the last four weeks, just to get a good average. If people are self-conscious about this, you can designate a recorder who will keep the absolute numbers to themselves. Then, week by week, whoever has a bigger *percentage* reduction of screen time wins that week. It has to be percentage reduction to be fair for everyone. You can also do social media absolute time or percentage reduction. You can do daily instead of weekly. There are ways to switch it up. You can also do this with as few as one other person. If you choose to do this as a group, make sure there are prizes (little fun prizes).

The second is the *personal challenge*. This will definitely work better if you have someone keeping you accountable. But the point here is still the same. Average your screen time over the last few weeks. Then resolve to simply do better! To get that number down! Also, you can do it day-by-day, but compare apples to apples, so this Friday compared to last Friday. Then reward yourself appropriately when you nail it, but don't you dare get hypercritical if you don't. Lots of grace here! This is all about self-awareness, and I think you may find you will be less likely to pick up the phone unless you have a specific reason. And if that happens, mission accomplished!

Have a gimmick for yourself to help you when you are prompted to pick up your phone. I needed one after averaging ninety-two pickups a day for a week. Let that sink in a bit. I picked my phone up ninety-two times each day. That is five times for each of my sixteen hours. Yikes! While I was on vacation! How's that for not being present in the moment! That's a problem, but I think we all might be surprised at how often we grab our safety blanket, maybe just say something to yourself, for example, "I don't need it" or some other catchy phrase. I have a friend who says a simple prayer when he wants to pick up his phone for no specific reason.

Have fun with this! What do you have to lose? Feeling better overall? Less anxiety? Less false sense of urgency? You can literally tell the false sense of urgency that it is not worth picking up the phone for no good reason at this moment! How about sleeping better? How about having more discretionary time?

Remember, sixteen hours in each day. How are you using them? I really like this idea because you literally can't lose. That is, unless you have thought of a way to lose, because I have not. Worst-case scenario, you hate it and go back to the way it was before. You're no worse off. Best case scenario, you really like how you feel and you have more free time and you feel more free and less chained to the phone, and you'll connect more with others and feel more alive! And you are simply more present, which really is a good thing.

Please don't just change from one screen to another. Going from phone time to tablet time is not really helping. It is just redirecting your energy. Switching phone time to your desktop or laptop also doesn't count. Switching phone time to Netflix or TV, and you are missing the point, which is to be off screens a little more. I really think you will be surprised how this works. Maybe take a little of that time for silence and solitude. Or play a game, a card game or a board game or an outdoor game. Go for a walk or just sit and breathe.

The more we can fight to end our dependence on our phones, the freer we will be. Free to be creative. Free to be present. Free to rest and relax and recover and live. Then we will be more able to become our best self!

Chapter 9

A LITTLE OF THIS AND A LITTLE OF THAT. AND THE FOUR HORSEMEN.

"Living with anxiety is like being followed by a voice. It knows all your insecurities and uses them against you. It gets to the point when it's the loudest voice in the room. The only one you can hear."

--Healthyplace.com

want to introduce you to a concept that I call the Four Horsemen of my Apocalypse. In sports, the Four Horsemen got their name while being the four members of the backfield for the Notre Dame football team in 1924. They were coached by legendary coach Knute Rockne. How's that for a football name? During their three years at Notre Dame, the Horsemen lost only two games. They simply won. They asserted their dominance. They trampled other teams.

The four horsemen of Eric Recker's apocalypse (and I suspect many more of you as well) are worry, fear, stress, and anxiety. And they have asserted dominance in my life. The more I choose to feed them, the more they run wild over me. The frustrating thing about them is that they have no power unless I give it to them. And they are really four rather terrible things.

The more I allow the false sense of urgency to have a foothold, the more I suffer from worry, fear, stress, and anxiety. The worse I sleep. The more jittery I am. The less able I am to sit still. The more I am consumed by needing to do something productive. It stinks, and it is preventable more times than not, but it is difficult to manage. My pastor today said this: "If fear is dominating your life, may I humbly ask what voice you are listening to?"

Are you watching a lot of news? Are you aware of how news works? Take a story and triple the sensational factor, then build it up more and more, and then put it out there to make people feel fearful, worried, anxious, and stressed. But keep them in a position where they have to stay tuned and learn more so they can't turn it off. Add a ticker across the bottom and an anchor who sounds really urgent, and you have a recipe for disaster, right?

Seriously, ask yourself: How much news am I watching? How much news do I need to watch? You may say, well, "I need to be informed. I am not going to be one of these people with their head in the sand not knowing what is going on." Okay, you may need to be informed, but what is happening inside you as you attempt to devour hours' worth of news? What is happening on a physiological level? What is happening to your brain?

Are you totally calm? Are you totally peaceful as you watch? Do you literally feel the cortisol (stress hormone) coursing through your bloodstream? Do you enjoy the news? And why do you think you enjoy it? And do you really enjoy it, or is it just something you do? It breeds anger in many of us. It breeds rage. And rage is addictive as well. So we watch more. And get more angry. And rage on!

Some may truly enjoy the news, but from countless conversations since COVID-19 hit, I have heard so many who are weary of the news and many who have shut it off altogether. They are not putting their head in the sand by any means. They are aware that if they need to know something badly enough, it will trickle its way down to them. They may not be the first to know, but is there always an advantage in knowing bad news first?

And many find themselves with a greater amount of peace once they decide to shut it down. You do you. You must discover for yourself what is the right amount of news or social media or Netflix to watch. For me, personally, I shut the news off in April. I didn't watch a lot, but I sure did peek at the Apple News app often. I deleted it. I could sure go back to it, but at almost eleven months without it at this point, I think I am good. And I haven't missed out. I have had people tell me all I need to know. And I get emails that are filtered specifically for news stories that relate to my profession. That's all the news this guy needs. But it took some self-awareness to get there.

Just pay attention to the things that cause worry, stress, anxiety, and fear in your life, and do whatever is in your power to limit your exposure to those things. Oh, be careful, little eyes, what you see! Oh, be careful, little ears, what you hear! Who and what is influencing you, and is it positive and affirming or negative and fear-based?

We have all had a day where all is good and we are rolling

along. Confidence and joy are up, the sky is blue, and everything is working out. We are feeling the flow. Then we get a message or see a headline or check our stocks or get some news or check something on our phone, and all of a sudden, our joy is gone. Just learn what things cause those responses in you and avoid them if you can!

If you are feeding the Four Horsemen, you are fighting a losing battle. Trust me, they are strong. They lost only two games! And they are scary. They are never satisfied. You can be completely beat down, with no hope, and they still want more ground. So don't feed them. Learn about yourself. Become your best version. Don't feed the false sense of urgency!

Now is probably another good time to discuss the benefits of seeing a trained mental-health professional, counselor, or therapist. The things I talk about in this book ring true for me. So I am sharing them, but I am not a mental-health professional. They are the experts here. I don't know your specific journey, and while I would be glad to discuss it with you and offer any insight I may have, please seek one of these great people out if you need to.

Have a discussion or many. Take back some of the ground to which the Four Horsemen have staked their claim. It does not belong to them. It is your ground, not theirs. You just gave it to them, and so have I. And just to be clear, I have seen a counselor, as have all of my family. We don't hide behind it. We are all very interested in becoming our best selves, so we do what we have to do to get there. And as for the Reckers, having someone to listen to us at different pivotal times in our lives has been nothing short of priceless!

We felt like failures the first time we made the appointments, but that was a gigantic lie. We weren't failures by any stretch of the imagination. What is bad or shameful about someone offering an objective approach to helping you do life better?

Remember early on when we discussed how no man is an island? This is so true! Don't allow yourself to become an island, to become isolated, to be in that place where you are all alone. It is tough, especially right now, with the uncertainty in the world. But we need others. We need friends. We need trusted advisors.

I remember feeling alone and isolated when my best friend (and unfortunately at the time, my only friend) moved away the summer before high school started. That was thirty years ago, very much pre-Internet. It was a devastating loss to lose a best friend. We have not talked since he moved away. It was a crushing blow, but there were better times ahead, and I was forced to put myself out there to make new friends. That was nearly impossible.

At that point in my life, I was an introvert through and through. And it is hard for introverts to put themselves out there. But you are faced with a choice: continue to be an island and wallow in it, or change it for the better. Talk to that coworker and see if they want to hang out. Join a gym or a yoga group or a club, or go to a meeting or a few, anything to get you around other people. I am confident that by the time this book gets out, there will again be some options for people to spend time together with less fear of a virus. We simply won't be able to go on forever in this 2021 "virtual" world. It is not sustainable.

The first step is always the hardest. That is why it is step number one. It is also the most important, because you can't have the next step without it. It will get easier, but it will also take some work. Figure out the life you want to live, preferably free from the false sense of urgency, and then see what it takes to get there. What obstacles are in the way? What needs to change?

Be realistic, but I am giving you permission to dream. It is okay to dream. We still just get the one shot at this life. It is simply not practical for me to dream about becoming a professional baseball player at forty-three, having not played baseball since I was fourteen. It is completely okay to dream about having a bigger impact, more joy, more quality relationships. It's okay to dream about peace, certainly yes to world peace, but I am talking about your own peace, the kind that crushes the false sense of urgency and gives you full permission simply to breathe in life.

Take the first step. Grab a piece of paper and a pen and sit down and either type or write (you know which one I will choose!) out "What Life Could Be Like" at the top, and then commence dreaming. Write it down so you can see, it and then tell someone about it. Then find out how you can make it a reality and live your best life!

This part is nonnegotiable. You get one chance at this life. You get one shot. You can't buy another turn with all of the gold in Fort Knox or all of Jeff Bezos's Amazon money. Just one chance. Please do not wake up twenty years from now or even one year from now with a bad case of the what-ifs. Or, as my Dad has always said, "Never should on yourself." He never wanted to hear from us kids that we should have done this or that. You are here right now. Own it and move on. Learn from mistakes, fail forward, and keep on going. Don't dwell in the past. We are here now!

Make a decision and own it! Live this life without regrets. Unless you have a terminal illness and won't make it through the next few hours, you still, in theory, have some time. So what are you waiting for? Do you want to live the rest of your life in restlessness, always feeling like you should be doing something but can't put your finger on it as it nags and nags? Is this the life you have dreamed of? Are you making a difference in the lives of others? And even better, are you making a positive difference? Do you want to? Is there something more to this life? Figure it out. One step at a time. Start out by writing down what it could or might look like.

Will you take ground back from the Four Horsemen and live boldly and confidently, or are you destined to live a life of defeat and discouragement? I know what I want!

One life. One chance at it. You got this! I believe in you. The million-dollar question is, "Will you believe in yourself?"

Chapter 10

SWIMMING UPSTREAM
(THERE IS A TIME
FOR THIS)

Remember, a dead fish can float downstream,
but it takes a live one to swim upstream.

—*W. C. Fields*

When I was engrossed in triathlon, I had to learn to swim efficiently. And faster. As I moved up distances from Sprint (500-meter swim) to Ironman (2.4-mile swim), it behooved me to learn to swim efficiently. It has been said that you cannot win an Ironman in the swim portion, but you certainly can lose one with poor or inefficient technique or a variety of other reasons.

Disclaimer: I was never even a little close to actually winning an Ironman race, but I wanted to get the point across.

The bottom of the pool never changes, and the winter months of swim training were mind-numbingly boring for me. And in Iowa, you mostly get winter months to train. Outdoor swimming is, at best, a three- to four-month opportunity. Back and forth. Back and forth. Fifty meters per lap. Longer workouts could be 3,000–4,000 meters, so that is sixty to eighty laps, back and forth. How does one break up the monotony and maintain reasonably good form? I am not sure I really ever figured that out. Sometimes I prayed as I swam. Sometimes I counted strokes. Sometimes I could actually zone out and let my body do its thing—that is, until I would forget my lap count.

Needless to say, I was thrilled when the lazy river opened up at our local aquatic center! We could use the lazy river as lap swimmers from noon to one, so I could really only go on Fridays, but I looked forward to it! There were walkers who wanted to walk against the current for greater resistance and swimmers who wanted to swim against it to get stronger.

And me, I just wanted a break from the bottom of the pool. But it was tough for a numbers guy like me, who always tracked the total swimming distance for each workout. I couldn't do that in the lazy river, and I would get out of there with very few "laps" to my credit, but mentally, it was a great boost. It wasn't an easy swim by any means, but it provided variety, and I truly loved the change of pace. And it was outside and not inside at 5:00 a.m. I would actually get excited to go swim in the lazy river instead negotiating with myself as my alarm went off to get out of bed to go swim laps.

Obviously, it is harder to swim against the current as opposed to swimming with it, but that is the point: it makes you a stronger swimmer. You time yourself around the lazy river and set a base time and then try to beat it. Then you try again. And try again. Of course, we all tried to beat each other's times, but mostly, our goal was to try to improve our own times. And then, when you are in a race and there is no current, you go faster and you finish faster.

It is this way as well with baseball. You swing a bat that is heavier or has a weighted donut on it in the on-deck circle so that when you pick up your lighter bat to actually try to hit a pitch, the swing will require less effort. You swim against a current so it will be easier in the race. You study hard so the test will be easier. You practice your speech so you feel comfortable and it is easier when you are in front of the crowd and the house lights are turned down and the spotlight is on you!

Sometimes, life feels like you are swimming against the current in the lazy river, and sometimes, you are turned around and swimming with the current. We rarely swam with the current in the lazy river, but it was an absolute blast when we did! With the current it is pretty awesome as you make great progress, cover many laps, and get your numbers up. Swimming against is harder! It can be less rewarding because you covered less ground, but you got your heart rate up, you got stronger, and you accomplished something that challenged you. Swimming with the current can almost be like coasting. The pressure is off. Less effort, less heart rate, less work. But it is also beneficial at the right time.

Isn't all this a lot like the false sense of urgency? The false sense is like constantly swimming upstream against the current but never getting there. No intervals. No breaks to breathe. No chance for recovery. Never finishing, as there is always something more nagging, pulling you in, grabbing your attention, and being relentless with its demands on your time.

Please don't hear what I am not saying here. Urgency can be okay. There was certainly an urgency in March as we tried to figure out the right initial response to COVID-19, and certainly, some of that was okay. There is urgency as a stay-at-home mom tries to get her children out the door so they don't miss the bus or she doesn't get them to school late or as she tries to get dinner finished on the table at a certain time. And the working mom trying to get her version of those same tasks accomplished. There are work and presentation deadlines. There are times when projects and assignments must be turned in. And some of that is okay. There is urgency as a big meeting that has been planned for a long time counts down. There is urgency in trying to catch a plane if you are running late and you hear that familiar announcement, "Last call for boarding," and once the door is closed, it will not reopen.

And the later you get in your college career without choosing a major, there becomes a real urgency to choose that major and make some kind of a plan for your life. And there is urgency as you have to have a difficult conversation and you feel ill-equipped and ill prepared to have that conversation as you consider the fallout.

Urgency is okay. It drives us at times, pushes us at times, helps us meet deadlines. It keeps us on our toes and hopefully keeps us from slacking off. It is the urgency of seeing two seconds left on the game clock when you are down by two points in a basketball game and you happen to be the clutch three-point specialist for the team, so you know your number is being called. It is the urgency of a test or homework deadline or a project or a presentation that needs to be turned in on time.

But urgency simply cannot be there all the time. It's a road to nowhere. Some urgency can create low-grade anxiety or nervous energy, which can be just fine and maybe even productive. The anticipation of a big day at work or a blind date or a presentation can all cause a level of response, from some nervous energy to all-out panic. You simply cannot run on urgency all of the time. Your mind needs to relax a little, not be so switched on or amped up all the time. You need to swim with the current once in a while to balance all the times you are swimming against it.

For all the times you are amped up with a list of a million things to do and you find your heart beating out of your chest and you can barely breathe and you are bouncing around from this to that at a pace that could only be described as breakneck, for all of those times, you need some other times. And those other times you need to be less switched on. You need to be less overwhelmed. You need to run on less adrenaline.

The false sense of urgency is not sustainable. And how might I know this? What expertise do I have to make myself a self-proclaimed expert on the false sense of urgency? To make it clear, I am not an expert, but I have lived through it a lot.

Every day, with few exceptions, over the past eighteen years of practice, four years of dental school, and three years of undergraduate school, I have gone into the day with somewhere in between a high level of nervous energy and full-on panic. I have had days when I have had to sit in my vehicle in the parking lot for several minutes trying to talk myself into the building. What is waiting for me? What messages will be on the answering machine? Who will need some of my extra time today, of which I almost invariably have none? Which procedure will be harder than anticipated? Which patient will test me? Which staff member will test me? Which piece of equipment will break today? Which patient will decide they don't like us anymore and go to another office? So many unknowns. And so much worry, fear, anxiety, and stress.

Then I would arrive at the office at 6:30 a.m. or earlier for an 8:00 a.m. start, and I'd stay until 6:00 p.m. and work on paperwork and charts through lunch. Not sustainable. And I was fully aware that it was not sustainable, but I pushed on. I forged ahead with no regard for anything other than this is what I felt I had to do. I didn't yet understand the false sense of urgency and its influence on my life.

The false sense of urgency told me that I had to keep going, even though I didn't know its name. I didn't even know what I had to get going on. And strangely, I would often look at what I had accomplished outside of chairside dentistry and see that, for the most part, I was thoroughly engrossed in busywork and had probably checked my email forty times. And to make it worse, as I was leaving, I felt this sense that there was much to do the next day and to make sure I came in early and got a good start, as there was much to do. Wake up with urgency, work with urgency, and leave with urgency. Too much urgency!

But for me, the false sense wouldn't relent. And it still hasn't. I would have a hard time unwinding so I could be a dad when I got home from work. When work literally zaps 100 percent of your strength and you still have other responsibilities as a husband, father, triathlete, and board member, something has to give. For me, it was often sleep, and sleep is not a good thing to give up, as you will pay for it at some point!

Sleep is a beautiful gift we are given. It is in sleep that our bodies attempt to heal from all the bad stuff we have put in them and to heal from the bad things we have done to them—poor posture, poor nutrition, overstimulation of our brains. And it is a time for our minds to heal, especially if we have been switched on all day. Sleep is to be a shalom of sorts, a time of peace.

So here I am, a dentist, husband, father, triathlete, board member, friend, and so on, and I am smoked. Can anyone relate? But I continue to listen to the false sense of urgency. You can do it! Just keep working, pushing, not sleeping, and running yourself into the ground. We were not designed for this!

But I didn't know any better, and so I kept listening. It actually took a pandemic and the closure of my dental practice for two months to see what the false sense of urgency had been coaxing me toward while I just passively agreed to its demands.

We get into a rut, and we just keep doing what we are doing. We get up. We go to work. Or now, maybe we take a few steps to work. We fight the same battles, internally and externally. We have the same fears. We try to get through the day to get home exhausted, just to do it all again. We can't wait for the weekend or whatever days we have off, but when it gets here, we have all these projects we think we have to do. Or a second job. Or a weekend full of sports tournaments for kids.

We have relentless to-do lists (or honey-do lists, as we call them). We need to see this person, go to this event, mow the lawn, finish the bathroom remodel, clean the house, go see this movie, go visit this family member. And let's be honest, does any of it really give us any joy?

I was at that point. Eighteen years of practice, and not very many breaks in those eighteen years, at least not breaks for rest. Sure, I went to India for almost two weeks to see the great work that a group called Mission India is doing in country, but that wasn't a rest-and-respite trip. Yes, I took two weeks as I climbed Kilimanjaro in Tanzania, Africa, but again, not a restful trip at all. And there were many other trips and continuing-education classes and meetings over that time. But when did I take the time to do some serious soul-searching about what I wanted in this life? You just work until you retire, and then what? I have had countless conversations with people on the verge of retirement or who have taken the plunge, and believe me, you better get that "then what?" part figured out. I have seen couples put all their eggs in one basket and scrimp and save and retire with hopes of travelling and seeing the world only to have one of them get sick or disabled and all for naught. They are stuck!

And while we are on it, get used to asking yourself the question, "Then what?" Let's say you get that sports car or Jeep or truck you really want. Then what? Let's say you have been studying for months for an exam and you push everything to the side and you pass the exam. Then what? You got the promotion at work and with it the monumental level of pressure and stress and new responsibilities. Then what? Are any of these things all you had hoped for? Or does the luster fade into reality rather quickly?

My point here is this: there will always be that question. Then what? When will it ever be enough? I asked myself those questions so many times while my practice was shut down and I actually got a break. And yes, I know, some of us got a break and some got other things. Some were actually considerably busier. Some got to work from home and were able to ditch a commute that had become a major time sink. Some all of a sudden felt their profession was under attack.

The answers to the "then what?" questions weren't satisfying for me. I started watching continuing-education videos and attending Zoom calls when I was off and quickly became addicted to these. Early on, I would watch three to five hours of videos a day on many of the days. Why? The false sense of urgency. I needed to do something. Going from full days of dentistry hunched over patients all day to very little structure was a real challenge. And it was a breeding ground for the false sense of urgency.

I needed to do something. I needed to learn something. I actually got more than a hundred hours of continuing-education credit over the COVID-19 shutdown and the following few months. And then what? Pushing to get more letters after my name? And why? What does it even matter?

But I did learn to kick the false sense of urgency below the belt a little during the COVID-19 shutdown. Left to my own devices and in full-on allegiance to the false sense of urgency, I may have watched seven to eight hours of continuing-education videos/ Zoom calls/ webinars during this time. But a strange juxtaposition happened. I had put so much pressure on our trip to Spain over spring break for my son Blake's senior year. Then, in a flash, it was gone, and I was devastated. We were going to watch a bullfight, take a day trip to Tangier, Morocco, eat Spanish cuisine, stay in a resort with a view of the Mediterranean, and so many more things.

I needed that trip. I needed it to connect with Blake before he went off to college. The sands of the hourglass were running through my fingers, and I was powerless to do anything to slow them down. I had put so much pressure on that trip. So much urgency. And now I had a choice. I could have wallowed in that feeling a lot longer, but early on, I realized this: those who chose to try to learn what they could from the COVID-19 time instead of wallow in it would emerge victorious. The others, those who focused more on what they lost than what they had, not so much.

So I rediscovered time with my family in both a quantity and quality way, and it was amazing. We had a multiday—actually, multi-week—game tournament where we played croquet and bocce and *Mario Cart* and every imaginable card game and board game and darts. And we went for drives almost every night. The boys would drive, and I would sit in the back seat with my bride, and we would just take it all in. And we went to get ice cream together, and we got take out together and we made meals together. We ate a load of ice cream! I think ice cream drive-throughs did *very* well during the pandemic! And we connected, talked, laughed, smiled, and loved.

And we had incredible time together. Before COVID-19 was even a thing, I was terrified of Blake going to college. Now I just simply know that he is ready and that it is good. I am excited for him. And as I write, he is in college and doing very well. And it is okay. He will do great. I am so proud of him!

My answers to the "then what?" questions got him to school, and so I realized I needed to put the time in with him before he left—not in an urgent way ("This time has to be super-significant and special") but in a more relaxed process ("We have today. Let's make the most of it"). And it was worth it.

My family is phenomenal, but I had gotten lost pursuing schedules and production and numbers and patients and staff and goals that, even when reached, kept me asking, "Then what?" There has to be an endgame to all this striving for it to be sustainable. You can't just robotically go and go and go forever.

I was thankfully able to do a midcourse correction in being

a dad to my kids. I am not sure I would have realized fully the need for it without COVID-19. I am not in any way thankful for the virus and the havoc it has produced, but I am very thankful for the lessons I have learned because I took the time to learn and ask, "Then what?"

And yes, parenting and being a spouse and wearing all the other hats that need to be worn is often swimming upstream. It is hard work. But it doesn't always have to be. I have met very few people who have the ability, over the long haul, to be always switched on, ready to go, and fired up, and not suffer the consequences of that level of urgency.

So swim upstream when necessary. Check off the urgencies that need your attention but only after careful consideration of which things are worthy of your attention. Do these things, by all means, because your job depends on them. (Or at least your keeping of your job depends on them.) And delegate the things that need to be done but could just as easily be done by someone else who might have a lighter load than you. Stick with the activities you are most productive doing. For me, that is chairside patient treatment. The other things are best accomplished by one of my very capable teammates. And when I delegate tasks to them, they realize that I trust them with important details.

Just don't let yourself listen to the false sense of urgency. Those things that are not important are not important. If you tend to find yourself constantly engaged in things that provide no answer to the "then what?" question, may I humbly suggest that you may be feeding the wrong animal. It is a slow, complicated, insidious process to become a slave to the false sense of urgency, and we often realize we are there after it has a death grip on us, but there is hope and healing to get out of it.

So tell it no. Focus on the things that matter. Much more on that to come later.

Chapter 11

HOW DO I DECIDE WHAT TO DO NOW?

One day you will wake up and there won't be any more time to do the things you've always wanted. Do it now.

—Paulo Coelho

So how do we decide which things are important? Which urgencies are legit, and which are like Oscar Mayer bologna? Here a few suggestions.

First, consider this: will the thing that seems so important in the here and now matter in five minutes, five hours, five days, five months, or five years? The more it will matter over time, the more important it is here and now, and the more it demands your attention.

Having the right dinner party with all the details is certainly important, but it is not nearly as important as having the right home or the having the right friends. Having a good presentation is important but not as important as considering how it fits into the long-term plan. And it is certainly not a reason to push everything else out of the way. And the presentation will never be perfect, I promise. No amount of work will ever make it perfect, so at some point, you just need to let it rip.

Do a little soul-searching on the long-term impact of whatever the urgency seems to be, and decide if it is worthy of your time. Is it worthy of someone else's time (can it be delegated?), or does it need to be discarded? Please remember that delegation to someone who is qualified to use their time on this project is completely fine. Just be sure that in lightening your own burden and taking something off your plate, you are not tying an anchor onto someone else's boat. Think of time here. Things and tasks that will not matter over time may not be worthy of your time.

Second, is this a busy-list item or a trajectory item? A busy-list item is something that is done out of obligation or possibly even perceived obligation. I need to clean the house right now. I need to do the laundry right this minute. I need to run to the store for this item immediately. I need to clear my inbox or at least make it seem not so menacing. I need to get my office organized, and suddenly that rises to the top of the priority list and you have no reason for why it escalated.

Truthfully, these things probably or possibly need to be done, but do they *have to* be done right now? These may be better categorized as things we want to get done. We all know people who never sit still and are tormented by the tyranny of the urgent. The second they sit down, they have to get back up and get busy doing something that might seem trivial to the rest of the humans in the room. Oh, he doesn't sit very well. Or she is not a sitter. They have to be doing something. Have these people waved the white flag and surrendered full-on to the false sense of urgency?

On the other hand, a trajectory issue or item is important mostly for what could happen if it is not addressed or completed. If I don't prepare for this meeting, I could lose my job. If I don't study for this test, I might not pass this class, and then I will have to retake it, and that is a domino effect, and you can see where this is going.

Take a little time and ponder the importance. I would get bombarded with busy-list items that I quickly accelerated to the equivalent of trajectory items and pushed more important tasks aside. The wild hair I would get to organize the lab and organize models and organize my office, while it truly needed to be done *at some point*, came at the expense of not writing up charts or returning patient phone calls to follow up. The need to organize my entire office, *today, right now*, was a lie and a well-disguised, desperate attempt at claiming more territory by the false sense of urgency.

Third, how will this affect my life and the lives of those around me? Again, I go back to the cleaning and organizing of my office. The urge comes, and it is strong. It is an okay task and worthy of my time and energy at the appropriate time, but as it becomes all-consuming and other more important tasks get pushed away, we have a problem. That decision affects the lives of the people who might be waiting for a call-back regarding their treatment. Just as an aside- I always made the calls, I just pushed them back in favor of the tyranny of the urgent.

I would describe many of these urgencies as things that just pop into your mind and steal your heart and rise to the top of the priority list. Fifteen minutes ago, this thing wasn't even on your radar, and now your whole being seems to be about it. One day, I was having a conversation with a patient, and I heard about a new road bike that was being made by my favorite bike company at the time, Specialized. The bike was called the Venge, and it was a pretty sweet ride. My heart was stolen, and I spent most of the rest of that day looking at bikes online instead of using my energy to get caught up on things.

It happens, and it happens quickly. Don't let these things that pop up out of nowhere get you off course. That is, unless, they really are important!

Fourth, consider contentment. I could write an entire book about contentment. And, God willing, I plan to! As the famous song by U2 goes, I still haven't found what I am looking for. Contentment is an elusive, fickle mistress. We have been sold a line. We are duped into thinking we are simply one purchase, one thing away from happiness and contentment. But the lie detector says, *That is a lie.* I remember watching Maury Povich growing up, and I remember all the lie detector tests and all the people who tried to live their lies until they were exposed. It was humorous but actually quite sad when Maury revealed there had been deceit. It was easy to laugh, but you couldn't help but feel bad for the people whose lives were on display and in shambles.

Contentment is not found in the purchasing of another thing. Believe me. I have done research and bought many things. Carbon road bikes, carbon triathlon bikes, Jeeps, Swiss watches, baseball cards, photos, and on and on. None of these things have ever delivered on their promises. Contentment is the antithesis of the world and especially of the American economic machine. If we had a country full of content people, the economy would be in utter ruin. But that does not mean we shouldn't try to discover a life of contentment.

So what is the false sense of urgency driving us toward? What is the endgame? And if you get this thing or this experience or this trip or this house or this car, any of the things you long for, what will it ultimately do for you? A content person, one who has, in fact, found what they are looking for in life, is much less focused on the false sense of urgency because they have found peace. They do not need to continue to chase all that stuff. They have self-awareness.

That does not mean a person who has found contentment is passive. Not in the slightest. It just means that the content person has sorted through some of the bull and has a different endgame than continuing to chase the wind, the next high, the next thing. It is a good thing to aspire toward but a very difficult thing to achieve. Victories in contentment come in small packages, but the cumulative effect is worth the work.

Fifth, be very careful of the lies our minds tell us. Our mind is a terrible office. Our mind is a terrible place for thoughts to go to die. Our mind is for things that matter and for processing life. Whatever thoughts we have that we need for later need to get down on paper or in an app in your phone where they can get out of your mind and not bog it down. David Allen talks about this concept extensively in his *Getting Things Done* series, a very solid series of books on productivity.

As I have been writing, things have come to me at the strangest of times, and often when I am lying in bed. I have a notebook I use to capture these thoughts, these seemingly random bits of information that make their way into my processing space. I have found that the false sense of urgency can literally crush you because as a whole, it is all way too much. But often, when you are overwhelmed by all the urgency, if you simply get it down on paper, it isn't so daunting. The list is almost always shorter than it seems in your head!

The tasks that seem impossible in our minds can quickly become much more manageable in list form when they are out of our heads. The mountain seems scalable, so that you can actually get ahead of this thing and you can really look at things one at a time. You can see which ones are high priority and which ones can wait. One thing at a time. And sooner than you might realize, you have conquered the list.

And no time is this more apparent than when you are trying to fall asleep. Keep a little notebook beside your bed, and when something pops into your head, you can either get it on paper or let it stew in your mind all night. I have even gotten very good at writing in the dark without having to turn a light on. And then I can get right back to sleep or maybe even just get to sleep. You can deal with that stuff tomorrow when you have more energy and the wherewithal to process it.

Sixth, here it is: our mind is such a tricky place. One minute, I find myself concerned about the possibility of having to step away from dentistry if life would happen to throw me some type of a health curveball and the economic ramifications. And the very next minute, literally the next instant, I am worried if I will win an auction for an expensive baseball photo. All of this can happen within five or ten minutes or even less.

This explains the urgency to become as profitable financially as possible so I will be fine should I be forced to step away by life circumstances and then use the large amounts of money I have been blessed with to buy stuff that further amplifies the need to work harder and longer. It's a vicious cycle. Oh, contentment, please come quickly. And the vicious cycle simply repeats.

And the world is full of people who are in a false-sense-of-urgency rat race to retirement, to travel, to see the world, to fish, to do woodworking, to volunteer, to live the easy life, to play pickleball, to work somewhere else part time, to sit in a recliner and watch tv, read books, and so on. The day is circled on the calendar for years. And then, when that day finally comes, the day that has been on the calendar for years, what is there? And *then what*?

Trust me, this is true. I have had so many conversations with my patients about this. We talk about the countdown to retirement and the inevitable "then what?" question. And then the day is there, and they have made it, and all of a sudden, they or their spouse or their friend gets injured or sick or can't retire yet, and then all plans change. And then all deals are off, and then what? And what if a pandemic hits months before retirement and that nest egg doesn't look as hearty as it did a few years or months ago?

All that hustle. All that worry. All that planning. All that false-sense-of-urgency rat race, and you find yourself smack dab in the middle of a life you hadn't planned for and you hadn't expected. And then what? What will you do? How will you react? Will you become bitter, as if life owed you something and it didn't live up to its end of the deal? Will you find yourself even deeper in the tyranny of the urgent?

And what if you don't find yourself loving all the stuff you were hoping to do with your retirement? What if you can only play so much pickleball or do so much woodworking? And what if you get kind of sick of books and there really isn't anything good on TV?

How about this: don't let the false sense of urgency and all the planning and preparation rob you of the moments right now that give your life flavor and meaning in exchange for what might happen someday. Maybe take a few trips here and there. Live life to the fullest. It doesn't have to be extravagant. I am just saying that if you spend all your life living for retirement and all the anticipation, is there a chance that it might not live up to the expectations? Remember expectancy versus expectation. Kind of makes sense, huh?

Life is moments. It is. Life just can't be all about "Someday we will do this thing." You get all this urgency focused toward someday and all the expectations that go with it. Is your heart prepared for the fact that your someday might not come?

Don't forget about what is in front of you. Be present. Don't be somewhere else. You cannot have the moment in front of you if your mind is on the next thing. So put the phone down. Have a real conversation. Take a day off here and there and invest in relationships. Vacation time is made to be used and not just accumulated. Take a little longer vacation that is not programmed and see what a preview of this retirement might look like.

Even do it spontaneously. Leave yourself open to what might happen. Expectancy says, "Let's see what happens. Let's be surprised. Let's see how it goes. Let's have a little flexibility." Expectation is about control and having everything ordered just the way you want it. The crummy thing about expectation is that if all of it follows through perfectly as planned, there is often no emotion or celebration because you expected it to go that way, kind of like retirement or the change to a new job. It should be a celebration or an excitement, but a lot of that depends on your expectations.

Expectancy is beautiful because of what might happen. The possibilities are wide open. The most content and happy and joyful people I know don't set a whole lot of expectations. They may say they are ready to retire, but they are going to take a little time to see what comes of it. They hold onto their plans loosely. And then, after they have been at it awhile, they may discover what they want to do with their time.

So what if we looked through life with a different lens of searching for contentment and living in expectancy? What if we left a little time for moments and allowed ourselves some grace to not have every minute planned? We can be so hard on ourselves, and we can make our lives so complicated.

What if we had discretionary time and the wisdom to use it well? What if we didn't just arrive safely at retirement but found moments, waypoints along the journey, that provided a whole lot of flavor to our lives? How exciting could retirement be then? Or would we even be so focused on getting there if we were caught right in the middle of living our best life without the false sense of urgency? Remember this: One life. One shot at it.

And this life is not lived on our phones. At least the good

moments are not. Not the real, flavorful moments. But if we don't allow space for life to happen, it won't. It will quickly pass us by. Do something spontaneous and wild. Take a random last-minute day off. Take your spouse or friend or child for a weekend away. Surprise them. Write a book. Or write a sentence. Dare to believe your best life is available. Your best days can be ahead of you. You just have to grab hold of life.

Chapter 12

BE A MIRROR HOLDER
(A.K.A., STAN'S WISDOM)

Always have a willing hand to help someone,
you might be the only one that does.

—*Roy T. Bennett*

L et me tell you a little bit about Stan. Stan is my mentor. Stan is my friend. Stan is 6'8" so he towers over me. Not many people tower over me, as I am 6'5" myself, so Stan is uncommon in that way. But the reality is that Stan is unique in many ways. He is one of the wisest people I have ever met, and that is saying a lot. It is a true joy to be in his presence because he very well might be the best listener I have ever met. When you are with Stan, you matter 100 percent. I have never seen Stan touch his phone when we are meeting together. I have never caught him checking his watch or looking off into the distance, dreaming about being somewhere else. Very simply put, Stan is the kind of person who lets you know you matter. He is the kind of person you want to be around.

Stan has defeated the false sense of urgency. At least he has defeated it in the sense that he is fully present. And I am not exaggerating. He is an exemplary human, and I have learned so much from him. I continue to learn from him, and I am always excited for what else I may learn from him.

Stan and I usually meet once a month at the Sports Page restaurant in Pella. He always shows up early for our meetings. He drives nearly an hour so we can have lunch each time. He shows up early to my office and is always waiting patiently. I tell him that I will be ready at 12:45, as that is when my lunch is supposed to start. I have clearly romanticized the idea that I will be done by 12:45. I rarely am done by then. It's a Murphy's law type of thing. It is usually at least 12:55, and I am running up the steps after doing a speed change, like Superman. And we head over to the restaurant after I apologize again for being late.

Stan has a way with people. The waitresses at the Sports Page can sense something different about him. He is a gentle giant who genuinely cares. It isn't a front. It isn't bull. He cares and it shows. I miss Stan. We hadn't met in person since the first week of March 2020 because of COVID-19. I missed his hugs. I missed his presence. We have done the FaceTime thing and phone calls, but it isn't the same. I couldn't wait to see my friend again. I hate this virus because it prohibited me from seeing my friend. I am so glad to be back at the Sports Page with Stan. Life just feels right when we get together.

Stan has shown me some critical things in my life. He very quickly picked up on my need to always be doing something big and my uncanny knack to run myself into the ground. He has been my mentor through joyous and painful times and everything in between. His encouragement has been huge in this book coming to fruition.

Everyone needs a Stan in their lives and sorry, you can't have mine. He may have some other availability. You would have to take it up with him. He is absolutely an inner-circle kind of guy. A trusted advisor. Stan knows me. He knows about me. He advises me without giving me advice. As he would say if you asked him, all he does is hold up a mirror.

Being a mirror holder for someone else is one of the best gifts you could possibly give them. A mirror holder is not judgmental, not hyper-critical, and not cynical. A mirror holder is not there to point out flaws. We are really good at pointing out our own faults. The world is super-judgmental on its own. We simply do not need more people judging us. A mirror holder does exactly what it sounds like. They hold a mirror for another so that the another can see their life through a different lens.

What does holding a mirror look like? Well, one goal is to help someone become self-aware of the things, patterns, mannerisms, and strongholds in their lives. We talked about self-awareness earlier, but as a review, the more self-aware you are, the more you know you. What you truly want. How you really feel. What your real motives are. These are tough things to figure out so here is how he does it.

Like I mentioned, Stan is present. You get the feeling, because it is true: there is nowhere else on this earth where he would rather be. This is absolutely mandatory. You have to listen, so he listens actively. He ponders and then asks fantastic questions. He was the first to point out if maybe, possibly, I still hadn't found what I was looking for after my first Ironman triathlon. He suggested that I ponder whether the end justified the means or whether I was simply chasing after the wind seeking the next high and the thing I was looking for.

He asks questions like, "How did that make you feel?" And then he encourages me to share with others what I need in a certain situation. It is amazing when you are honest with people about what you need out of a relationship or in a situation. How do you feel, and what do you need? Honesty is refreshing and needed in our current culture. It is not in any way selfish. It breaks the ice and shows them you are genuinely interested in becoming your best self.

I say all of this to encourage you to be a mirror holder but also find someone who could be your mirror holder. Don't worry if you don't have someone that pops up in your mind to be yours. This is a big part of what counselors and therapists do. And it is okay to see a counselor. Many people even have mental-health benefits with their insurance to help absorb some of the costs.

And the great thing is that you don't even have to be great at giving advice. And you don't need to have a lot of wisdom. You just need to listen and ask good questions and you can learn how to do that. Just make sure that the other people in the room are your top priority. Get in the habit of not letting your mind be elsewhere. You can do this. Don't overcomplicate it. And yes, there are feelings involved. Get over it. It is okay to talk about feelings. If you can't talk about how you feel, how do you expect anything to change or to make any progress?

I know what you may be thinking. I ain't going to see a shrink. That's for sick people and messed-up people. Well, as I said before, all four members of my family have seen a counselor. It is okay. Sometimes, it is just good to unload on someone who is a confidential good listener. My wife and I felt like total failures when we sent our boys to see a counselor, but the results were priceless. They learned a lot about themselves and about their life and their identity. Please consider it if you need it. Preferably before you really need it.

You have to be present to be a mirror holder. You can't be somewhere else looking at your phone or zoned out to whatever is next. The person across the table from you or the person you are talking with on the phone deserves that. They deserve your undivided attention. And which of us couldn't benefit from becoming a better listener? I know I could improve.

The other concept that I have learned from Stan that I treasure is this: drawn versus driven. Stan asked if I was drawn to triathlon or driven to triathlon. Was I drawn to climbing Kilimanjaro, or was I driven there? Was I drawn to completing my FAGD/ MAGD (designations/ advanced degrees from a dental group I belong to)? Was I still drawn to being a dentist and business owner, or was I driven to continue my profession?

The difference is simple but not easy. To be drawn to something means it captures your heart. It excites you. It gets you out of bed in the morning. It is simply something you want to do. You see it as something you get to do. For me, it is things like writing, playing games with my family, praying for people and sharing life together, taking walks with my wife, going out to eat, collecting baseball photos, driving to get ice cream, and getting lost on a gravel road with my bike.

Think of being driven as an obligation. I need to do this. I feel as if I have to do this. It is my duty. Now lots of driven things really need to be done, and so they are not at all bad. Week sixteen of a forty-week Ironman plan felt much more like driven than drawn. My tenth six- to seven-hour mountain bike ride in preparation for Leadville was driven. No drawn whatsoever. The studying for the test to get my fellowship in the AGD was driven. Wow. I really am not a fan of studying, but it was the next logical step. Getting my pilot's license- drawn. Studying and taking the test- driven.

And speaking of taking tests, I vowed never to take a test after

I walked out of the University of Iowa College of Dentistry for the last time as a student. Well, how's that working out? My FAGD required a test. My private pilot certificate required a test. And there will be more. Never is a long time so how's that going, Eric?

I am driven to go to work, to produce, to lead, to mentor (well, maybe drawn and driven on this one), to move through the schedule. I am drawn to relationships. I am drawn to share my life with my team and with my patients. I have a tendency to be an open book. I am drawn to bike rides to and from work to help cleanse my mind and prepare or decompress from the day. I am literally driven to go to work each day.

I think it is important to discuss the things in life we are driven to. Can those become things we are drawn to if we pivot a bit or change course slightly or significantly? If our lives are full of only things we are driven to may I humbly suggest that our lives may not be full of much in the way of joy. I am going to guess there is a correlation between affliction by the false sense of urgency and the balance of drawn/driven in your life.

Too much driven leads to less joy and more false sense of urgency as you try to compensate for being engrossed in something that does not bring you joy. Being more drawn leads to more joy and less urgency. I suppose you could also get in trouble by having too many things you are drawn to. You might become a person who gets distracted a bit easier but I think that is a bit unlikely. And if it does happen, I would much rather be on that side of the equation, by a mile of landslides.

As we are humans and not robots, we can only handle the driven for so long before we become a shell of our former self, way less than our best self, and cruising (slogging) through life with little to show for it other than a burnt-out human who is stuck and can't get out. We simply need to have some things we are drawn to. It might even start small, by listening to a few podcasts to find out what you like. As I mentioned before, I suggest Jon Gordon's *Positive University* podcast or Bob Goff's *Dream Big* podcast. We all need positivity in our lives, and Jon Gordon has it in spades. He is the positivity guru, but he wasn't always that way. He had to overcome a lot of negativity to become the positive leader that he is today.

But whatever you choose to be drawn to, do not let it be negative. Especially if you are in a rut, don't make that rut worse. Don't camp out anywhere near the news even if you think you are drawn to it. The news takes and takes, and you get very little for your time with it. I was actually going to open Twitter the other day. Twitter has been what I would consider a dumpster fire, a disaster, since COVID-19 hit. And I suspect it has been that way even longer. I just look at it now with different eyes.

The words that rang in my ear as I was about to open it were this: "as a dog returns to its vomit." Right. I know that is gross, but it is true, and it brings home the point. Oh, be careful, little eyes, what you see. It's a garbage in/garbage out kind of thing. We can't expect good results in our life if we fill it with garbage, and news, by and large, is garbage. I apologize if that is not a popular opinion, but I have found it to be true. Nothing good came from my time on Twitter, so I gave it the ol' heave-ho. I may go back, but if I do, who I follow and why will become much more important.

Just be careful. Even what you are drawn to might not be beneficial for you. You may be drawn to online shopping, but it may be mounting up credit-card debt. You may be drawn to the casino or sports betting, but it may be ruining your family. You may be drawn to golf, but six hours every weekend may not be in the best interest of your family. I was drawn to triathlon at the start and there were no doubt some really great health benefits, but all those hours put a strain on my business and on my family.

At some point, drawn turned to driven, as I was defined by triathlon. It became my identity. And when something becomes your identity, you feed it, and it becomes even more what defines you. So be careful how all-in you go on things, especially things that seem benign at first but may take a lot of time from your sixteen hours per day. Count the cost.

So hold the mirror for someone else. And by the way, this does not mean that you wait until they are done talking and blurt out what they should do. That is entirely something different. All you were doing was waiting for your turn to talk. Not good—unless they ask for your advice. Even then, please tread lightly, as words are powerful.

Drawn or Driven?

Take an inventory of how you spend your time and your money. You need some things you are drawn to, or you will burn out. Trust me. Eighteen years of pedal to the metal with predominately driven activities is hard on a mind and hard on a body, as stress is sustainable for only so long. But oh, the four horsemen love to be fed, and they need to be fed. Don't be afraid to talk with someone, especially if you are just stuck.

And I hope you find your Stan, a person you can be truly real with and with whom you can share life. And try to be a Stan for someone else. Make their life better. We are all in this together. One life. One chance. Go do it!

Chapter 13

FEAR AND THE URGENT

One of the best lessons you can learn in
life is to master how to remain calm.

—*Catherine Pulsifer*

F ear is brutal. Period. Fear, unfortunately, drives a lot of our decisions. Fear just happens to be one of the Four Horsemen of my (and many other's) apocalypse. Fear takes and takes. It never gives you anything except for an adrenaline spike that will invariably lead to a crash as that spike is simply not sustainable.

Okay. Yes, I know there are some of what may be considered "healthy fears." Things such as fear of water as a little kid keeping you from drowning. The fear of a hot stove prevents you from touching it. The fear of losing your parents keeps little kids (sometimes) close to parents in public places. It certainly, however, does not account for the time I wandered away from my parents in a shopping mall when I was in preschool, but that's another story altogether. Don't worry, my mom likes to make sure I don't forget. The fear of getting caught has derailed many a nefarious behavior before being carried out. Yes. I am very aware of these. This is not what I am poking at here. I have had those healthy fears as well

We all have fears that drive us and determine our trajectory to some extent. If you, for some reason, do not, then I applaud you, but I do not necessarily fully believe you. There are myriad fears common to people. Depending on which year you choose, here are some lists from the wonderful world of Google. A 2019 survey of 2,000 people showed the top ten fears, in order (bibliography 1):

1. Snakes
2. Heights
3. The dentist (believe me, having been one for eighteen years, I know!)
4. Confined spaces
5. Needles (yep, also me)
6. Clowns
7. Public speaking

8. The dark
9. Flying (also me, as I am a pilot)
10. Birds

Here is a 2014 list from the *Washington Post*. Hey, at least a dentist didn't make this list! Oh wait, except for needles and blood. How's a guy to win with this list? (bibliography 2)

1. Public speaking
2. Heights
3. Bugs and insects
4. Drowning
5. Needles/blood
6. Claustrophobia
7. Flying
8. Strangers
9. Zombies
10. Darkness

So there you have it for me: I am a dentist. And spoiler alert: I use needles. And hey, I am a pilot, and that also covers heights. So I am involved in four out of ten on the 2019 survey! Yeah me! It is tough being in a profession in which so many people readily vocally express their displeasure. People genuinely don't want to see me. There was even a joke shared with me once after several women had said they would rather give birth than come to see me for treatment. Cleanings are fine. Just avoid my chair at all costs.

Here's the joke.

A woman says to her dentist, "Hey, Doc, you know I would rather be pregnant than be here."

The dentist says, "Well, you had better make up your mind. It depends on how we position the chair!"

I know, it's a little cheesy, but it's a real joke. I have heard it a lot. And believe me when I say I have heard every permutation of "I do not want to be here."

Very few days have gone by when someone hasn't said to me or my assistant that they didn't want to see us. We even had a spectacular doozy of a day about fifteen years ago. My assistant of eighteen years at this point (three years, at the time) noticed that our first patient didn't want to see us. Not a big deal or abnormal, as most don't want to see us. This continued, and we chuckled when the third person in a row said the same thing. By lunchtime, the streak was alive and well, and we wondered if we might have a full day of it.

Lo and behold, our last patient of the day arrived. We were waiting with bated breath, and he sat down and said, "Ya know, Doc, it's not you guys personally, but I am really not looking forward to seeing you!" We burst out laughing. How could we not? But that is my reality. And it wears on a person, no matter how positive you try to be.

If the best you are hoping for out of an appointment is for the patient to say, "Ya know, Doc, that wasn't all that bad," you have set the bar pretty low. And that is our reality. And it's okay. I feel a higher purpose in my job than simply fixing teeth. I am much more about relationships and getting to know people and sharing life, and in the process of doing that, we just so happen to fix teeth once in awhile.

We talk about it all the time in our office. Relationships will last. And of course, we want teeth to last. But sometimes they don't despite our best efforts, and we desire to be in relationship with as many people as we can be!

So what do you fear? And what does that fear do to you? When everyone says they don't want to see me, it makes me fearful of seeing them sometimes. And it ain't getting any better since COVID-19 showed up, not by a long shot. I have found that fear creates urgency or builds upon the false sense of urgency and makes us prisoners.

If you are fearful of something, does that fear encourage confidence? Does it lead to courage? Does it spur you on to action? Will you directly go after the thing that invokes fear and get it out of the way? Or will you push it to the side for later and let the urgency and stress build in a cancer-like fashion?

If you are one of those who first checks off the most overwhelming, stressful, fear-provoking item off your list, I salute you. Keep doing that! That is not the norm. I feel like the normal course of action is to push it off to the side. It seems safer there, except it isn't. It festers. It nags. It creates urgency that builds on the urgency that you already feel. It is a lot.

So what drives you in life and in your vocation, whether you are a CEO, a dentist, a custodian, a stay-at-home mom, a car salesman, a cashier, a host/ hostess, a taxi driver, or a retiree? Here are a few fears that I would argue create urgency, the false urgency that nags at us and won't let us relax and be present and enjoy this life, which we have been given as a gift.

The fear of looking bad. No one wants to look bad, so we strive for perfection, which isn't attainable. But we lie to ourselves and say we need to be perfect anyway. That way, no one can see our weaknesses. And then, when we weren't perfect, who saw us? What is going to happen? It is a vicious cycle that we can't get out of.

The fear of not being prepared. For a test, for a presentation, for a meeting, for a dinner service (have you ever seen *Hell's Kitchen*?), for a spouse who is on their way home, expecting the house to be in order when it has been ransacked by tiny humans. Here it is: we will actually not be prepared sometimes for every contingency or even for one contingency. We simply cannot be everything to everyone, and we can't know what expectations they have if they don't share. So we can't live here. It is a horrible existence.

The fear of running out of money. This particular fear plagues people who are near retired or retired and find themselves on a fixed income that doesn't go as far as they thought it would. Maybe you retired too soon for your own comfort zone. So what now? And maybe you are just figuring out that your lifestyle is inconsistent with your salary and you are stuck with a mound of debt.

The fear of losing control. No one here struggles with this one, right? We all want a little control, and some of us want a lot of control! And we fear what happens if someone else is placed in charge, for example,

> if our child makes bad decisions we can't control
> if the meeting steers away from our agenda
> if a decision is made that is not in our best interest
> (or at least we perceive it that way)

The funny thing about control is that it is an illusion. We never have it to the level that we think we do or want to.

Fear of "then what?" We talked about this question earlier. There is so much anxiety about what is next.

> What happens after retirement?
> What will I do after high school?
> What happens after college?
> What if I can't find a job or if I lose the one I have?
> What if I get fired?

We can plan and plan and plan, but at the end of the day, how many of our best-laid plans come to fruition? The more you are attached to an outcome, the more your world turns upside down if you don't get that outcome. In life, one thing is certain: there will be a "then what?" There is always a next step. Is that okay with you, or does it inspire fear and anxiety?

Fear of the future. Again, back to planning. The unknown can cause a lot of urgency. The future is uncertain, and it can seem very urgent to plan. I went through more than five plans for returning to seeing patients after our COVID-19–mandated shutdown. The final draft was a thing of beauty, all laid out on brown paper, 7 feet by 12 feet and all written out. We had a five-hour staff meeting about it. And guess what? It changed. And it will change again, and probably again. The future is coming. And chances are it will be different from what we expect. And that is okay. The more we fear it, the more urgent it becomes, and the more we are stuck.

The fear of Monday. Does anyone struggle with this? We just got into the weekend grove and the peace that comes with it, and now it's back to work. Back to the grind. That's a kick in the teeth! How do we handle it? Do we start getting moody at some point on Sunday? Do we have trouble sleeping on Sunday night? Does it hit first thing Monday morning? This one is real. Believe me. Or was the weekend chaotic because of tournaments and commitments and we actually look forward to our routine coming back?

I have struggled with the fear of Monday since the second or third grade. Find out what it is specifically that you fear about Monday. Is it facing coworkers? Is it a project that is due? Do you simply hate your job? Are you stuck and Monday is nothing more than a reminder of your current state? Is it going back to routine after a couple of days off? There is a reason. Because fear of Monday creates an urgency that, ready or not, it is coming. How awesome and beautiful would it be to break free from this one, to be able to simply see Monday as a different day, a new opportunity instead of a fear?

Fear of sleep (or lack of sleep). This one is pervasive. In 2016, *Consumer Reports* estimated that Americans spent $41 billion on sleep aids and sleep remedies, and that number was expected to climb to $52 billion in 2020. And a conclusion—these "solutions" everything from sleep gadgets to supplements—found that not all of them are worth your money. *Shocker there!*

Sunday night can be fraught with restlessness. So what do we do? We medicate with sleep aids or food or alcohol, and our sleep hygiene is terrible (we will discuss more on this later). We have to realize that sleep is a process and know which things help and hinder sleep. Alcohol and sleeping pills may seem like a good idea, and they can get you to cash out, but what they do not give you is a restful night of sleep. They just help you pass out.

So ponder this with me if you will: we all have things that we are afraid of, or at least cause us some apprehension. What percentage of those things we fear actually happen? NBC News (bibliography 3), on December 3, 2017, said that 85 percent do not actually happen. This was in a segment called "How to Worry Better." Wait a minute, how to worry better? What does that even mean?

A Penn State University study (bibliography 4) had participants write down all their specific worries for ten days. They were to write down the source of their worry anytime worry started to creep in. They then reviewed those lists for thirty days. The results of that study: 91 percent of the worries were false alarms. Even out of the 9 percent that did actually come true, the outcome was better than expected one-third of the time. So, in reality, six out of one hundred actually happened. Six percent. And one-quarter of the participants had zero worries materialize. Six percent, or roughly one out of sixteen worries. I will take those odds. But there is something about our mind that tries to assure us that the thing we are worried about is in that 6 percent. The mind is a dangerous place.

Therefore, fear is a liar. Worry is a liar. So why are we so captivated? Why are we so fixated? Why are we so negatively focused? Why do we live our lives believing a 6 percent chance of something happening? And do we have to? Is there a better way?

The false sense of urgency loves fear. With a passion! Our fears drive us to feed urgency with a buffet of actions. Let's take the fear of Monday. Monday is coming. It is inevitable. There is roughly a 100 percent chance of Monday happening. So what is the real fear? Fear of going back to work? Fear of failure? Fear of the unexpected (as in, what is going to happen this week or this day that will be horrible?) Fear of routine? Fear of not getting enough sleep and being behind the eight ball? Just as I said before, we have to get to the root of the worries and discover the rationale for worrying.

Fear causes either fight or flight. Fight means we engage it and we are going to stand in and kick Monday in the teeth. And there is urgency about it and we prepare and over-prepare. Or there is flight. We avoid it, deny it, and pretend it isn't going to happen. We medicate for sleep, and we have alcohol or we binge eat or binge watch or binge phone or binge scroll (those are not really terms, but you know what they mean, and you know we do it!)

Six percent. We need to acknowledge our fears for what they are. They are distractions from life and from the task at hand. It's really quite simple. So much of my personal fear, worry, anxiety, and stress stems from an eight-year-old boy who has realized he isn't good enough to get picked to play kickball on the recess field at school. It is that same eight-year-old boy who is pushed down, has his backpack taken away, and is teased by the bigger kids, the bullies, on his way to school. And it continued through middle school. He's just not good enough. He has a last name that is almost too easy to make fun of and a total lack of self-confidence because he has been shown he isn't good enough. When that little boy doesn't believe he is good enough and simply can't overcome, a monster is created that believes the six percent. That was his reality, and he believed it, and it festered. And even though life changed and things got better, he spent his teens, twenties, and thirties believing he still wasn't good enough. And so he had to over-strive to prove himself to everyone. But it was never enough.

But here is the thing: he was good enough. He is good enough. He was created on purpose. He has value, plenty of value. And he is just like everyone else in the sense that he is just trying to figure out where he fits in the world. At forty-three, still searching, still fighting the 6 percent, still struggling to believe but making progress. Seeing a light at the end of the tunnel, realizing so many things through self-awareness.

I bet many of you can say the same thing. Maybe have a similar story. But there is hope—hope to conquer the 94 percent and also the 6 percent and endure if the 6 percent does come true.

Are you created on purpose? The answer is yes, but do you believe it? Can you make a difference in this world? Again, same answer. Do you have value? Do you add value? Are you trying to figure out where you fit in the world? Is there something bigger or more impactful for you? Will you choose to step out and believe that 94 is almost sixteen times greater than 6? That's about as good as I get at math. It's not my strong suit.

There are a lot of yesses in the answers to these questions. I will put it bluntly: if you don't believe that the answer to these questions is yes, then I want you to talk with someone who can help convince you otherwise, because no one will believe in your potential if you don't. Fear will take and take and take. You need to go on the offensive and take some of that ground back for the good guy.

This isn't all rah-rah stuff. This is real life. The life that is meant for you is out there, and if you are living it, then I applaud you and hope you are very thankful for such an opportunity. If you are living your best life already, that is an incredible gift, but if you are not, you must believe that it is out there and you simply cannot believe the fear. The statistics are what they are. Six percent. Gamble with those odds. Live life with those odds. Take those odds to Vegas. Vegas would be broke or never would have been built if the odds were 94 percent in your favor. But the reality is that Vegas is not broke.

They are killing it—or at least were before COVID-19. But overall, they are winning because it isn't a fair fight. And that's the way it is with fear. Fear gets to be relentless and punishing if we let it, and when we believe it even a little, it ramps up and festers and overwhelms us and tricks us into believing much worse odds than 6 percent.

This is true during COVID-19, and I am sure the same will be true after it calms down a bit, that fear will still be rampant. And the media is the worst. All mainstream news outlets that I know of are guilty on some level of sensationalizing the news to increase fear. It's what they do. I fix teeth; they create hype. The more sensational, the more fear, the more glued to it all we are— the more clicks, the more money. It's all a bit out there if you ask me, which you did not.

I hate fear. I hate what it does to people. But there is hope. There is a lot of hope in our best days being ahead of us. But we have to choose the hope. It will not choose us. Mindset is so important. If we believe it is all going to be rotten, it will be. But if not, anything can happen. There is hope in the journey of becoming the best version of ourselves, not someone else's best version. Don't go there. Don't even try. It's not as glamorous as you think. It never is.

Sometimes you may even need to play out the worst case scenario. My wife and I have done this before when we have something that we are apprehensive about. We talk and discuss what is the worst thing that could happen. We actually go there. And we usually find one of two things. First, that worst thing might not be as bad as we had originally thought. And second, if it actually happens, we have discussed it and are prepared. But the majority of the time, it is all overblown and doesn't end up anywhere near as bad as we thought it might.

So dig in for the ride. If you are willing to take the first step, fear might just become a thing of the past, and at 6 percent odds, I am thinking it sure should be.

I am a visual learner, so this helps me.
Or here is a pie chart if you need it.

Fear vs Reality

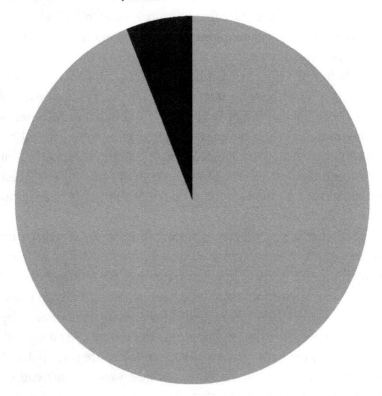

6%

May happen, probably not as bad as
you think

94%

Not gonna happen

Chapter 14

THE THRILL OF
THE CHASE

The Art of Fulfillment is the ability to
experience not only the thrill of the chase,
but also the magic of the moment, the
unbridled joy of feeling truly alive.

—*Tony Robbins*

Have you ever wanted something so badly that you pursued it? You thought about it. You researched it. You learned about it. You borderline stalked it. It maybe even nearly put out a restraining order on you. Your mind was absolutely drawn to it. You wanted it. And sometimes, you even ended up getting it.

And then what? Was it worth it? Did it leave you feeling as good and fulfilled as you had hoped for as you were chasing it and pursuing it? Or did its luster fade, maybe before you even got your hands on it or soon after you got it? Or was this thing everything you ever hoped it would be, and is it still? (This is rare, by the way. It is actually quite uncommon for something to live up to expectations over the long haul.)

If you repeatedly seek things out (especially material things) and believe they are going to be everything you hoped they would be, you might just be a victim of the thrill of the hunt or the thrill of the chase. You actually may be more interested in the pursuit than the result of the pursuit.

What in the world am I even talking about? Well, you know me a bit by now and know that I tend to share a few stories, so here is another story. In 2013, I heard about a company called Starwood Motors. Maybe some of you have heard of them, and others may pause before you go any further and see what all the fuss is about. They are an exotic car/custom Jeep dealership in Texas, and they build some cool stuff. I mean really cool. I recently checked their website for nostalgia's sake to see what they are up to these days, and I found a $229,000 custom four-door Jeep. Wow! Just looking for about five minutes brought back a few of those old feelings—of when I lost my heart to those Jeeps and ultimately to one in particular. If you are a Jeep guy or gal or a car guy or just like cool stuff, take a minute to check them out. They are really cool. But also be careful. They get really addictive, as almost any Jeep owner can tell you!

From the first moment I looked at their website in 2013, I knew I had to have one. I gave my heart and mind to it. I had stopped triathlon in 2012, and apparently, this was more than willing to take its place in my headspace. I bet I spent over a hundred hours over a few months looking at specs and color and winches and lift kits and tires and agonizing over which one to buy. Kevlar custom paint, spotlights—so many choices.

After months of looking, obsessing, and being captivated by those Jeeps, I picked out the one. Gray Kevlar paint, all the options, exactly what I wanted. And just so everyone knows, the model I got cost a *small* fraction of the $229,000 rig I mentioned before. Think more like a new Jeep with some upgrades. Oh, and by the way, I live in Iowa, and Starwood is in Texas, so it was loaded on a truck. I sold my Jeep that I had and my car that I drove to work, wired the money, and it was on its way.

One Friday afternoon, my wife and I met the semi driver at a gas station right off the interstate, and there it was, strapped down and ready for me to enjoy. After almost four months of investigating, pondering, exploring, and searching, here it was. It was backed off the truck, I signed the papers, and I got the keys and was off! Windows down, tunes blaring, T-tops removed, wind in my hair. This was it. This was the payoff. This was the good life, the good stuff. And then, a warning light came on. Something about the front steering alignment. And my joy evaporated. The reality of my new toy set in; it wasn't what I had hoped it to be. So I humbly went to the local Jeep dealership with my new Jeep that I had not bought from them, and they fixed it for me. It was a slice of humility to pull in and ask for help. You would think a guy who has a Jeep that is that loaded up with gear like this one would know something about fixing it. Not me! Shoot first, ask questions later! I have never been a fix-it kind of guy. I am more interested in just enjoying the things I purchase. My bike mechanic, Kris, loves that about me! I keep his shop busy.

I ended up having a fair amount of fun with that Jeep. I pulled a few people out of the ditch or out of the snow with the winch. I had a really good time on snowy gravel roads, knowing that if I went into the ditch, I could just drive right back out. But I never took it off road. I never used it to its full potential because I was concerned that if I wrecked it, it had to go back on a semi trailer and back to Texas, where it would get fixed. And with 35-inch tires, it wasn't very fun at all on the highway. And Amy hated driving it. It rode very rough and everyone waved to her because they thought it was me driving. And she felt like it was one huge blind spot which made driving more challenging. And she was right. The Jeep stuck out. It was impossible to go incognito. Pella is a small town. If you aren't from a small town, then this part makes little sense to you. In small towns, we wave at each other when we recognize someone. I kept the Jeep for about two years, and then I traded it in to get a truck, a Ford F-150, which I still have and really enjoy driving. Amy will drive it without complaining, which is nice. I don't blame her for hating the Jeep. It was a tank. But I got duped, duped into thinking the Jeep that I wanted so badly was going to do something magical for me. It didn't. But at this point, I really didn't realize that I was a victim (self-imposed victim) of the thrill of the chase.

The thrill of the chase, a.k.a., "the grass is greener over there" or "if I just have this, then I will be happy, content, popular, satisfied, ready, etc." The thrill of the chase is when the pursuit of a thing is greater than actually getting the thing. The pursuit of the Jeep was actually greater than owning the Jeep. The vacation rental doesn't look like the brochure. The jeans don't fit the way you hoped. The watch isn't noticed by as many people as you had hoped. The weight-loss gimmick is just that, a gimmick. The new car suddenly has a rattle or gets a door ding in a parking lot. The picture in the new TV isn't as fantastic as you had hoped. And so it goes, on and on.

I think this is a huge thing with online shopping. When you finally click "buy," there is a sudden adrenaline spike as we commit to buy and pay. And often times, when the thing we purchased comes, there is a hollow feeling. Maybe it isn't the right color or it looks different than it did in the pictures. Or maybe it doesn't fit right or as you had hoped, or it wasn't as advertised. And maybe it is back-ordered for the foreseen future. Maybe it even isn't as big or as small as you expected, didn't do what you thought it would, or many, many other possibilities leading to disappointment and unmet expectations.

I wonder how many of us have gotten caught up in this from time to time. If I only get the promotion, then I will make more money and life will be good. Well, the promotion may provide more money for sure, but what about more quality of life? What about more responsibility? And do you really want more responsibility? Does more responsibility fit into what is best for your family? What about more hours? What about managing more people? What about it inevitably *not* being *everything* you believed it would be? Are you ready for that?

Finding out if you are a thrill-of-the-chase type of person is a part of your journey to self-awareness. It took me a long time to realize this. I own many things that I obsessed over before purchasing, and rarely did they end up being "as advertised" in my mind. My mind plays tricks on me and convinces me that I absolutely need this thing. I play along until I am in way too deep and virtually committed, and I usually end up getting it, because I know me, and I know my patterns.

This was also true of the Leadville bike race. It doesn't always have to apply to material things. I believed in my heart and mind that finishing this race would be an amazing thing. It would be a literal mountaintop experience. There was so much training and anticipation and follow-through. And in the end, the race-day experience simply didn't justify the sacrifice—the hours of training, hours away from my family, money spent on race entry and a new bike, and mental wear and tear chasing this thing.

I am not proud of being duped into believing that this thing would be more than it ended up being. But I am getting better at knowing this about me so that I can attempt to avoid it in the future. It's all part of my journey. It's all part of our journeys. And if my learning this about myself can help you on your journey then it is all worth it!

We must be careful about putting expectations on things or people. Earlier, I talked about living in expectancy versus expectation. Expectancy, if you recall, is living in a state of anticipation, of seeing what might happen and not having a lot of preconceived notions of how something should go. Expectation says, "I am seeing this event end this way or going this way, and that is what I want to happen or what will inevitably happen."

Expectation is dangerous because if you set high expectations and they end up coming true as you expected, you think, *Well, okay, that is what I expected.* Even though it may be a tremendous victory. So even if it ends up being a really great thing, there isn't much upside.

This is where perfectionists get in trouble as they constantly set themselves up for failure if everything around them is not ordered in the perfect way they have designed in their mind's eye. It is great to do your best, but let it go. We are imperfect creatures, and our work oftentimes will be imperfect. That is just reality, no matter how hard you try to fight it.

And as humans, we need to live with some potential upside. We need to be pleasantly surprised from time to time. We need to be wowed. We need an occasional smile on our face because something happened.

In relationships, expectations can be truly dangerous if not catastrophic. If you expect someone picked up your hint about a gift or a special event, then you set yourself up for a massive disappointment. Because you dropped hints but didn't actually tell them what you needed. And they, in fact, did not pick up what you were putting down.

A missed gift or a missed anniversary that was expected

to be otherwise is a huge disappointment, but in reality, who is to blame? I always tell my wife that I am super dense and not prone to hints. I suspect I may be a typical guy in this respect. I promise her that if she expects something from me, she better go ahead and tell me because otherwise I will surely miss it. This is a better way.

Don't have unrealistic expectations of others. They won't live up to them, you will get frustrated, and they won't understand why, and it really ends up being a case study in poor communication. Be honest with each other about what you need. You won't always get it, but at least it is out there in the open and there is no room for false interpretation.

On the other hand, Amy has told me that she doesn't like surprises. A win for communication and a weight off me, as it limits how creative I need to be. It does not, however, allow me to not try. I just have to be strategic.

Expectancy simply says, "Let's do this thing and see what happens." Expectancy is holding on more loosely to an outcome. See what might happen. It may be good, and it may be not so good, but you are opening yourself up for some major potential upside. Living in expectancy is the spice of life. Let's just go drive around and see what we see, see where we end up. This was a common theme for us during our COVID-19 shutdown. It was about what we could do. And we usually, but not always, ended up getting ice cream, which is pretty cool.

Let's call up that couple we wanted to hang out with. Let's just catch up on life. Let's see what happens. Reach out to a friend or family member you are out of contact with. And in a job setting— hey, I get to go to work today. I get to be around people. I get to influence or teach people. I get to learn today.

Expectancy versus expectation makes such a difference in our attitude. Entitlement goes along with expectation as we believe we know what the outcome is going to be and we expect it and feel we deserve it. Entitlement leads to disappointment if it doesn't go the way we feel we deserve. And that leads to pouting, which is a symptom of entitlement. Bad stuff. Expectancy goes with eagerness and suspense and sometimes the element of surprise. This sounds more joyful to me!

The thrill of the chase—how does this tie in here? What's the connection? We get attached to a thing we want or a new job we want to do or a person we want to date or be friends with. And the more we pursue, the more we become attached, the more we expect the outcome and set ourselves up to be disappointed when the thing doesn't live up to its hype.

We find ourselves being Clark Griswold in *National Lampoon's Christmas Vacation*. For those who haven't seen the movie, Clark is the dad who wants to have Christmas at his house with extended family. He sets expectations that no family event could ever live up to. And we do as well! We sabotage ourselves by living in expectation all the time. This thing is done this way and he or she behaves this way. And all of these things in my life happen in this order, at this precise time. There is nothing wrong with a plan, but being around someone who operates this way can be truly suffocating.

We need some joy. We need some anticipation. We need some expectancy. We need some room to be surprised, or else we chase and chase and chase and end up with exactly what we don't need and maybe even don't want.

Expectation fuels the false sense of urgency perfectly. Expectancy drains it and strips it of its power over us. Expectation when I wanted to buy the Jeep caused me to pick up my phone absolutely every chance I got to look at Jeeps, stressing and agonizing over every detail so it would be perfect and absolutely everything I wanted.

I am not saying you should just wing it. There is a place for rational expectancy, but it can't be your modus operandi. It cannot be your only way if you want to be your best self. The only way you can discover if you are a thrill-of-the-chase-type of person is through self-reflection, self-awareness, and introspection. But once you learn how you work, you can learn to take positive steps toward being who you want to be, reaching your full potential and crushing the false sense of urgency. Do you really want or need that shiny new thing? Or are you just chasing the thought of it and constructing a lie about what it might be for you?

Chapter 15

THE MYSTERY OF SLEEP

A good laugh and a long sleep are
the two best cures for anything.

—*Irish Proverb*

S leep, sleep, sleep. Those who never struggle with sleep are fortunate. I am envious of you. We have family friends who are sleepers. They can crash at any time and rest so well that we wish we were them! People who get a restorative night of sleep are miles ahead of those who do not. Poor sleep is tied to so many chronic-disease processes, from high blood pressure to type 2 diabetes to Alzheimer's and dementia to acid reflux, and the list goes on and on and on. Lack of sleep affects even our immune system. And in the middle of a pandemic, the last thing we need is any assault upon our functioning immune system. We need that thing to be firing on all cylinders in case we get sick. Not to mention frequent mental distress, also known as the false sense of urgency.

The bottom line is this: we need sleep, and we suffer without it. Earlier, we talked about usable hours of the day. Our sleeping hours can not be a consistent area to draw from to get more time if we want to thrive and be the best versions of ourselves. You can't just get more sleep the next night. It isn't bankable. It isn't cumulative. Well, you can get more sleep the next night in theory, but your body doesn't see it that way. We can't really bank sleep or borrow from sleep's time and expect good or even average results.

We need more sleep, especially Americans. We are not getting anywhere near the amount of sleep we need. According to the CDC (bibliography 5), one in three adults don't get the seven hours defined as "enough" sleep. I would call seven hours the bare consistent minimum for optimal health.

According to a Gallup poll (bibliography 6), we now get an average of 6.8 hours of sleep per night, which is down from an average of 7.9 in 1942! In addition, 14 percent said they get consistently less than five hours of sleep! And only 56 percent say that they got "as much as they needed." That is scary!

This lack of sleep is an epidemic and is costing our healthcare system a boatload as we care for people with chronic diseases. It is costing our companies insane amounts of money in lost productivity from virtual zombies walking around after a night of garbage sleep. I can't imagine this is getting any better as we work at home in our pajamas. The coffee and energy drink companies are killing it, however, as we make a feeble attempt to medicate with caffeine to overcome a putrid night of sleep. And it goes on and on, over and over, night after night.

Am I am expert on sleep? No, but I understand what happens when you don't get enough. I have taken continuing dental education on airway management and mouth breathing and its relationship to sleep, so I am not totally out in left field on this, so I can certainly offer my story as a basis to start.

I have struggled with sleep ever since I can remember. When you are scared to go to school, Sunday night becomes a warzone in the mind. When you are overwhelmed by work and it comes like clockwork on Mondays, Sunday is a dangerous night. And when you want to do long-course triathlon, you have to find the time to train. And if you want to see your family as much as possible, that training time needs to come, by and large, when they are asleep. And I couldn't train at night. I sort of turn into a frog at about nine thirty. It's time to seriously start contemplating bed at that time. My family jokes about it. "Oh, look, Dad fell asleep on the couch again!"

As I edit this part of the book, it is eight thirty the night after fall daylight savings time, so my productive time is coming to an end as my body is pretty convinced that it is nine thirty. And, oh, by the way, it is Sunday night. Yeesh.

I was someone who borrowed time from sleep to get things done. And I really didn't ever count the cost. I wanted the medals. I wanted the accolades. I wanted the Ironman tattoo. Nothing was going to get in my way. As the races got closer, you could see this kind of schedule for me.

Monday 5:30 a.m.	swim at the pool
Monday p.m.	bike ride
Tuesday 5:30 a.m.	swim at the pool

Wednesday 3:30 a.m.	3-hour run
Wednesday p.m.	bike (recovery, shorter)
Thursday 5:30 a.m.	swim pool or open water if warm enough
Friday usually 3:00 a.m. or 4:00 a.m.	start 6-hour bike ride
Saturday 6:00 a.m.	90 minute run for tempo
Sunday afternoon	60–90 minute bike

Does anyone see a pattern there? There are a lot of early mornings. And when I say that the swim is at 5:30, that means I am at the pool at 5:30, ready to swim. This means lots of nights falling asleep early or at least trying to force myself to sleep early. That always works, right? I ran on adrenaline so much for so long when I did triathlon. It's a wonder I maintained any sense of health. I am super blessed genetically, and that helps. But the false sense of urgency really blossomed in my fatigue and tiredness. I ran on adrenaline, as I said, because my body was trying to keep me rolling, to keep my mind sharp for my patients and simply to survive.

And by the way, the year I was preparing for my first Ironman, my kids were seven and four, and I had just assumed ownership of my dental practice and was heavily engaged in building a new dental practice with ten treatment rooms. Guess which of those things I did to the best of my ability? You are right—none of them. But I did just that: survive. No thriving during that time. How my wife stuck with me, I will never understand. She is an exemplary human being.

As soon as I let my guard down at the end of a workday, the adrenaline would run out, and I would crash hard. Or lie awake in bed for hours, unable to sleep. I never knew which one it was going to be.

So I started taking 50 mg of Benadryl nearly every night and did so for almost eight years. As long as I knew I would be in bed for at least six hours, I took Benadryl. And then one day, on vacation, I looked at my pill bottle of Benadryl and said this is ridiculous, and I quit taking it. At this point, I was done with triathlon, so that helped as well.

I now have a stronger cocktail that I take often on Sunday nights only, as I know there is a good chance I will lie awake for a long time if I do not. It takes the edge off. By all means, if you need a little help occasionally with sleep, please consult your physician. These are strong medications and should be used only under the supervision of a physician. But before you make that phone call to get an appointment, let's first discuss sleep hygiene, because sleep hygiene is super important. And the solution to a problem should not always be to medicate it first.

What exactly is sleep hygiene? It is the activities and processes around your preparation for sleep—the acts and events leading up to the attempt to go to sleep. It includes the time leading to sleep, the act of sleep, the area where you sleep, and pretty much anything associated with sleep.

The ideas and concepts I offer are simply advice and things to try. Not all these will work or make a difference for you. Not all of these work for me, either. But they are a jumping off point.

Because we need to sleep. Lack of sleep causes the four horsemen to ride with much less resistance. Lack of sleep causes us to have a massive false sense of urgency and rarely the amount of drive needed to carry out the activities necessary to complete our lists. A good night of sleep makes us think we can conquer the day so that the day doesn't stand a chance because we are at our best. Sleep makes us think we can, at a bare minimum, systematically make it through our day.

Lack of sleep makes us see not only the magnitude of what is ahead of us in a different light, but it also amplifies any interruptions to our day so that anything that pops up seems much less manageable and far more insurmountable when we are tired.

First—and I am just going to put this out there although I

know I will get pushback—we need to put our screens down. And I don't care which screen we are talking about. TV, phone, tablet, desktop, projector, or anything else with a screen is dangerous to the prospect of us getting a good night of not only sleep but actual rest and restoration.

The National Sleep Foundation (bibliography 7) recommends 30 minutes with no screen time before bed. Other studies recommend 60 minutes or even 2 hours of no screens before attempting to sleep. Okay. This is all well and good, but why? What is the science?

Screens stimulate our brain. We really do not want brain stimulation when we want to go to sleep. We want the opposite. We want brain relaxation. And the blue light that is produced by specifically screens blocks the production of the natural sleep hormone melatonin. And we need melatonin to start the wind-down process.

"Oh, but Eric, I bought those blue-blocker sunglasses so I can look at my phone or TV and then go right to sleep. The light doesn't bother me." Okay, fine, but I would caution you that those glasses are questionable at best in their effectiveness. And what about the brain stimulation? Did you solve that as well? Screens fool our brains into thinking we aren't just yet ready for a night of sleep and restoration.

I collect old baseball cards and old baseball photos. I mean really old—one hundred years old or more. Babe Ruth, Ty Cobb, Lou Gehrig, Honus Wagner. I really enjoy it. I have been buying fewer photos, as my collection has matured and as I have realized that I am a thrill-of-the-chase guy. But I like following the auctions. Okay. That's not completely true. I *love* following the auctions. The adrenaline spike seeing how my bids are holding up is a ton of fun. The dopamine feels good as long as I am just observing and not actually bidding.

There is one auction house, which just happens to be my favorite, that ends their auctions on Sunday nights at midnight.

Sunday nights just happen to be my worst nights of sleep. As I write this on a Saturday, tomorrow is actually the day this auction ends. They do three auctions a year, by the way. This is one of the few nights each year I sit with my tablet in hand as the time ticks down so I can follow my bids. And all the signs are there. My mouth is a bit dry. My heart rate is up a little. And the anticipation is palpable.

And guess what—here are the possibilities. First, I win what I wanted to win. I am overly amped up from the adrenaline and staying up too late and don't get to sleep for a few hours after the auction ends. The other option is this: I lose, and I am disappointed and can't fall asleep for at least an hour, maybe two. Third, I haven't bid but am still watching bids come in, living vicariously through those placing bids, and I am texting with some friends to see how their bids are holding up. And once again, I am all worked up and amped up, and I still can't sleep! None of these doors are a good option.

Screens are not conducive to sleep. This is why I don't keep my phone by my bed unless one of my kids is out late. It's why Amy and I and my kids do not have a TV in our bedrooms. It is why my kids (even my eighteen-year-old) are not allowed to have their phones in their rooms at night when it is time for bed; preferably, they never have their phones in their rooms. But that is an entirely different discussion and getting more complicated as girlfriends are now in the mix. Just consider this as a possibility.

Okay. We could talk about that in a whole other book easily, maybe two to three books. But for the sake of moving on, let's also talk about food. Everyone likes food, right? When I am ready for sleep, I want my body to be focused on one set of processes— rest and healing. That is what sleep is meant to do. Our bodily processes shut down other than the ones that repair the damage we did to our body that day.

We just add a bunch of things that interrupt those processes. Ideally, you should not eat three hours before bed. I know, I know, that simply just doesn't work for everyone. But it is a suggestion. And with all suggestions in life, we analyze them and see how they fit in my life. Why does it matter? The closer we get to sleep time with our food, the more our body has to focus on digestion instead of rest and repair and healing.

But what about me, you might ask? Many people get hungry before bed. I understand. I do sometimes as well. Just be very careful about what you eat. Eat a small piece of fruit, such as an apple or a banana. Or veggies. Or a glass of soy or almond milk. These are are easier to digest and can be eaten closer to bedtime with much less effect on overall sleep quality interruptions.

We do not want our bodies digesting a big bowl of cereal when we are falling asleep. It isn't conducive to good sleep. Or that bowl of ice cream. During COVID-19, we have gotten more ice cream than normal, but we try to eat it earlier in the night as opposed to later. If we have ice cream after 9:00 p.m., I know beyond a shadow of a doubt that my sleep will suffer. Or take that big bowl of buttered popcorn as you veg out on the couch at night. It's all tough to digest and diverts a lot of energy. So just be smart about eating at night after dinner. As I always love to say, make good choices!

What about alcohol? Sleep and alcohol have a strange relationship. Alcohol can make us tired initially, but it can disrupt our sleep as it wears off. It can also worsen snoring and sleep apnea, which affects the drinker and anyone who might be sharing a bed with them or attempting to sleep within earshot of them. As a general rule, it takes one hour to metabolize one serving of alcohol. So, if you have a few drinks, it is best to do so long before bedtime. I didn't say all of this would be easy to stomach or be popular, but it is science.

In addition to these few suggestions, a sleep mask may be helpful because it tricks your brain into believing it is time for sleep. It makes the room seem darker, and it may prevent dry eyes, if that is something you struggle with. Also, consider room-darkening shades as a bright room is not conducive to sleep.

Some may also benefit from an ambient noise maker or a white noise machine. Especially for those who seem to be light sleepers and wake up with any noise, this may help. My family sleeps with just a little white noise to drown out any other small noises that might wake us up.

So, instead of the phone or the TV or tablet or computer, what if you can't fall asleep quickly? How about reading a book? Just be careful here. A suspense thriller is likely not a good choice. And it is best not to read on a screen, as that defeats the purpose. What about journaling? I have, at different times, gotten into the habit of writing down five things that I am thankful for at bedtime each night. I keep a small notebook on my bedside table to hold these gratitude ideas. And I also write down things that are running circles in my mind so they stop running around. And then they are out of my mind, and I have a better chance of sleeping. Please, don't try to go to sleep with a full, busy mind.

Do not force yourself to go to sleep. Do not even try. If you aren't ready to go to sleep, it simply will not work, and you will be frustrated. You might lie awake for hours, which defeats the whole purpose. If you can't fall asleep, try reading or journaling, or just get up for a bit. Or just try to breathe slowly and sit in silence pondering the positives in your life or dreaming about the future.

Also, don't drink caffeine too late in the day. You may think it doesn't affect you, but studies suggest otherwise. If you tend to be a clock watcher, hide it so you can't watch it. Use an alarm clock that is not on your phone. I have a great one that vibrates instead of making noise so it doesn't wake up my wife. We have very different sleep requirements, and I like an alarm clock that wakes up only me.

Also, try to get to sleep at a similar time each night, with a similar routine. Your body gets confused if you are not consistent. Working through your routine will help your body know it's time to start shutting down for the day.

How is your mattress? It is important to have a good mattress and good pillows. We spend money on comfortable shoes and chairs and massages and chiropractic adjustments, which are all good things, but is your mattress conducive to a good night's sleep, or is it thirty years old, with its best days far behind? Some companies even offer a money-back guarantee to take the risk out of this costly investment.

Is your bedroom dark, cool, and well-ventilated? My family friends, the good sleepers, have box fans in every bedroom. The fans check two boxes: ambient noise and ventilation. How about blackout shades?

Exercise. You do not need to train for an ironman triathlon, but you do need to move. Stagnation doesn't promote good sleep. Ideally, do it earlier rather than later, but anytime is fine as long as you allow time to shutdown afterward. And exercise the right way. Get your heart rate up, then let it recover, and do it again. Interval training is fantastic and conducive to good health. Seek the advice of a personal trainer if you are unsure about how to start an exercise program. And make sure to check with your physician to see if you are healthy enough to get your heart rate up.

Stay hydrated! I try for a gallon of non-exercise-lost water per day. Loosely translated, I drink a gallon of water in addition to what I drink when I exercise. Yes, I visit the bathroom a lot! My body performs better when it is well hydrated. But I also weigh 225 pounds. A good amount to aim for is 1 ounce of water for every kg of body weight. Or, if you want to make it really easy, take your weight in pounds and divide it by two (cut it in half), and that is the number of ounces you should drink. If you weigh 150 pounds, then aim for 75 ounces. Yes, I realize that is a lot of water. And the higher you get to that amount, you may need a little electrolyte addition to stay properly hydrated.

Don't start with that amount tomorrow. Your body won't know what to do with it. Ease into it, and try to drink more earlier in the day unless you want to get up a lot at night. So, if you did really terrible at drinking water today, don't make up for it right before bed. And notice I said water, not coffee, not energy drinks, not caffeinated beverages. Water. Flavored water is better than nothing by far, and the electrolyte water is fine as well, but it really needs to be water. And if it is flavored water, certainly be aware of artificial sweeteners.

Your bedtime rituals and routines and nightly habits, collectively your sleep hygiene, are very important. Your body can only survive and thrive so long if it doesn't get a chance to heal and rest. Bad night of sleep after bad night of sleep leads to—you guessed it—worry, stress, anxiety, and fear. You know those guys. And it all compounds. Then the false sense of urgency attacks you relentlessly. You can't ever get back ahead of things without getting some sleep.

In the fall, we all see what happens to kids when they are tired. Friday night after the first few full days of school is ground zero for research. These kids are smoked from a week of stimulation, and they get irrational and combative really quickly. It is obvious they are wiped. Well, we as adults are just grown-up little kids. When we don't sleep well, we tend to see some of the same patterns emerging in us. We are just done. Fried. Smoked. Stick a fork in us.

Oh, shift workers, I hear you! I wish I had better news and better wisdom for you, but I know many of these ideas can still benefit you. Mothers of small children or single parents, I hear you. You are in a really tough phase of life, but lying in bed staring at your phone will not magically make it all go away. Endurance and the thought of how long this will last has to be overwhelming for you even on a good day. Do your best. Hang in there. Live life one day at a time. Remember, we only get one chance at this life.

And I realize there will be myriad excuses and many valid reasons why these principles may not work for you. I simply can't write a book that takes into account every single personal variation in life. This is simply intended to be a framework for a start at getting some better sleep and living your best life. I would ask you, however, to explore the reasons these principles won't work for you to see if they are valid points or excuses for staying on the same path.

How is this thing going to work if we keep the same habits and expect the results to be different? You may have to just realize that it just isn't working anymore. It may simply be time to try some new things. If it ain't fully broke, it may still need a whole lot of fixing, but that is for you to decide. Don't look back ten years from now with a wish that a few inputs had been tried. These aren't earth-shattering changes. If you don't seem to get any relief and have exhausted all of your options, by all means, make an appointment with a sleep specialist. There may be an underlying issue that needs to be medically treated. Try the suggestions I have outlined, but be an advocate for yourself. No one knows your body better than you do.

Do some research. Seek professional help—either mental health help or sleep help or both. Let's get to the bottom of this to help you become your best version, live your best life, and just give yourself a chance to enjoy life as much as possible!

One last thing to ponder here before we move on: What exactly is affecting your sleep? Can you pinpoint the source? For me, for a long time, it was the Ironman triathlon. For a while, it was simply an all-out fear of Mondays. When I stepped away from triathlon, my sleep improved noticeably.

You always have to count the cost of the ways that you spend your sixteen hours (or, in this case, your twenty-four). Is your job causing you to sleep less? And what part of the job is causing loss of sleep? Do you need that job? Is there another vocational option that might offer a better overall quality of life? Or could a small change in your attitude or routine at work make a big difference in your perception? Are you the mom of little ones that don't sleep well and so you don't sleep well? Is this really the time to try to add another child to the mix? Just process your day and take an honest look. Are there things or habits you have built in that are sabotaging your sleep?

Are you not sleeping because you are binge-watching Netflix every night? And what shows are you watching? Do they give you peace or cause you to get amped up? Are you not sleeping because you are anchored to social media all hours of the night? Sometimes, the answer is obvious; sometimes, not so much. And even if the answer is obvious, you really have to want to change. It won't happen on its own. This isn't an easy thing to solve or even to work on, but sleep, no matter how much you get, is a significant portion of each and every day, and not getting enough can sabotage you faster than almost anything else I am aware of.

Who is at their best when they are worn out, tired, or exhausted? I know of no one. And I have done lots of research. So put the phone down. Find a routine. Get some rest already. Better days are ahead, but we must believe they are ahead if we want to defeat the false sense of urgency.

Chapter 16

MY DUE NORTH

Knowing my True North gives me the
courage to focus my energy where I
believe it should be, not according to
what is popular or pleasing to others.

—*Jennifer Cummings*

L et me preface this chapter by saying this: you don't have to read it. The book is at least mostly complete without it. But to me, it has to be included for those who want to read it. I need everyone to have the chance to know this part of my story. For me, it's the most important part of my story, the anchor of my motives and values, the reason I am writing this book, my north star—the direction I look toward in all situations in life.

Read ahead if you wish, but don't let anything here diminish your thoughts about the lessons you have learned from the entirety of the book. Please don't be offended if we have different worldviews. We can agree to disagree, and that is okay. That is getting to be a huge and even bigger problem in our country right now: we can't simply agree to disagree. Everything has gotten so hateful and so polarizing, and so much discord is being sown.

We need to work through this, to listen to each other, to actually hear each other, and then and only then to share our thoughts in a nonjudgmental fashion. I have great friends on both sides of the political aisle, and the reason we remain friends despite our different political views is our mutual respect and love. We don't hate each other because we disagree. We need this in our country very badly right now.

Okay. Enough introduction. My due north is simply this: my belief in the Triune God: Father, Son, and Holy Spirit. And it is my faith in my Lord and Savior, Jesus Christ. This is why I can write. This is simply where my words come from. It is pretty wonderful. I sit down to write, put my pen on the paper, and the words start to flow. It is really remarkable.

And I am not sure if it would have started had I not been open to whatever God had for me during the COVID-19 shutdown of my practice. It is a funny thing when you have spare time and you are willing to sit and listen for whatever God may have to say to you. So I sat and listened, and the idea for writing and speaking was born. Remarkably, I was talking to a great friend about my future and what it might look like. I mentioned the term "false sense of urgency" to describe my angst over the last several months and the fact that this sense, this angst, has really plagued me for the majority of my life. He said to me, "Well, there's the title of your book. Write a book about that, and come work with me. I will put you in front of people who need to hear that message."

I had several conversations with people about the possibility of speaking and writing. I am told it can be a slow and painful process at times. It can take a really long time. But by the grace of God and His direction and words, it has not taken a long time for me. I am eight weeks into writing this, and the only limits to the words flowing from my pen have been the busyness of a job in healthcare and other life stuff that just gets in the way of going to town on this thing. And there's the struggle with deciding how much time to take away from other things to write.

God gave me the idea and the vision for this book. It was clear to me that this was the book I would write, and it was also clear I would write it from a viewpoint that it would be accessible to everyone. Equally clear was the directive to include this chapter to make it complete. It all just flowed.

Jesus is the true antidote to the false sense of urgency. Take a close look at this life. He wasn't in a hurry even though He knew his time was short. He had time for people, and He was present. Even if He was on his way to something important (everything He did and everywhere He went was important) and someone touched his robe and was healed because of it, He took the time to have a conversation with them. He validated them. He showed them love. Even when His dear friend Lazarus was near death, did Jesus drop everything and run to Lazarus? Would we drop everything and run to a friend to get another moment with them before they passed? We would try. Jesus remained where He was because He hadn't wrapped up what he wanted and needed to do. He stayed where He was for two days. He had more work to do, unfinished business. He knew His purpose. And he also knew His power. When it was time to go, He went. But He did not want to miss out on a divine appointment. Everyone and everything was important in the eyes of Jesus. He was not overcome by a false sense of urgency. He even knew He needed to rest and recharge, so He would withdraw to a quiet place for rest and prayer. He had figured out the mystery of a sustainable pace even though he was fully aware He had such a short time for ministry.

Knowing you only had a few years or months to live would probably cause most of us to feel a sense of urgency—urgency to make sure your affairs were in order, to make sure plans were made in an attempt to feebly control the days you had left on this earth. Not so with Jesus. He modeled perfectly how to defeat the false sense of urgency. He told Martha to focus on what was truly important instead of all the busy little details. He made sure His relationship with His Father was well-nurtured through quiet and rest and prayer. He cut right to the heart as His and the Father's chief concerns are the condition of our hearts, not just our outward appearance.

What is most important to us? How do we spend our time? What do we do with the sixteen and the twenty-four? How do we spend our money? How do we share our time and our talents with others? Do we find ourselves spending six hours a day on our phones and saying we don't have time for other things? Do we scurry around on our phones, unable to survive without them in our hands due to FOMO (fear of missing out)? Do we fear we might miss an email or a social media post or news headline and might not be the first to know or might not know at all? It is a real fear for many.

What if we miss someone's post? What if we can't be the first to comment or retweet or like? And what if we post and no one likes or retweets or comments or shares? What does this do to us? Does it increase our anxiety by a factor of ten? Does it increase our worry, stress, and fear? Do the four horsemen get fed when we are on our phones? You bet they do. But they may also get fed when our phones are within arm's reach and we wonder what is happening on them.

But we get just enough small dopamine hits that our brain is briefly satiated but not satisfied. And then we put the phone down. And then, like clockwork, almost a minute later, we feel like we *have* to pick it up again. Why? Because that is how phones and social media work. The developers are geniuses, and they figure out ways for us never to leave.

If they can keep us captive in their apps—whether it be Facebook, Instagram, Twitter, Snapchat, or TikTok—they keep their advertisers happy, and we spend money on things we didn't even know existed let alone wanted! And then we realize the algorithms they designed give us a skewed sense of time, and so we have to scroll through again after refreshing because we just might have missed something, and we certainly can't have that!

Jesus is the void we all have that no amount of money, nothing in social media, and nothing on the news can ever hope to fill. There isn't a car or a home or a vacation or a baseball card or a Jeep or a watch that can fill that space, no matter how hard we try and hope. There isn't a grade or a job or a child or a piece of jewelry that will fill it, either.

The void we have in our hearts, that constant uneasiness or angst that there might be something more to this life, is the God-shaped hole in our hearts. When Jesus isn't there, it feels a lot like urgency. If we just get this and this and this and this, then life will be good. If I just get this car or this Jeep, then I will be good. If we can just take this vacation, then it will be good.

But it never is! Never enough. Never. Never. Never enough. Jesus is the difference-maker, the way-maker, the forgiver of sins, the life everlasting. He has come that we might have life and have it to the full (John 10:10). He is light and life. He is perfection. And he is alive! And He is the reason for this book. Eric Recker is the earthly author and vessel for the writing, but make no mistake about it: these are the words given by God.

So, if you want to talk about Jesus some more, then let's talk. It's not difficult. It's actually quite simple, but it's not easy. I would love to show you why I have the faith I have. It can be a struggle day to day. I won't lie. But it is so worth it. Having Jesus in your heart as your North Star is the secret to crushing the false sense of urgency.

And as for the four horsemen—God was clear about how to deal with them.

Worry. Don't be anxious about anything, but in everything, by prayer and petition, with thanksgiving, present your requests to God. Then, the peace of God, which transcends all understanding, will guard your hearts and minds in Christ Jesus (Philippians 4:7–8).

Fear. Do not be afraid. A version of this is actually said almost 365 times in the Bible, so it must be pretty important.

Anxiety. "When anxiety was great within me, your consolation brought me joy." (Psalm 94:19).

Stress. "Peace I leave with you; my peace I give you. I do not give as the world gives. Do not let your hearts be troubled, and do not be afraid ." (John 14:27).

Let's get this thing wrapped up and look at some other ways we can defeat the false sense of urgency and start moving with the current for a while—or for good!

Chapter 17

ACTION STEPS AND HOPE (OR JUST HOPE)

Hope can be a powerful force. Maybe there's no actual magic in it, but when you know what you hope for most and hold it like a light within you, you can make things happen, almost like magic.

—Laini Taylor

S o here we are, the home stretch, approaching the end of the line. If you have stuck with me this far, I would like to offer you a few things that might help you in your journey. And remember this always- it is in fact YOUR journey. It is not someone else's journey. Let them have their own journey, and don't let the circumstances of anyone else's journey muddy up yours.

Remember this next phrase well: the grass is actually seldom greener on the other side of the fence. We have a tendency toward comparison. We just do. And we think as we look at someone else's polished Instagram-perfect life, if we only had that life, we would be good. No more worries. Well, I have news for you. People typically don't post the crummy parts of their life on their Instagram page. They post the stuff that makes others envious and jealous. They post the look-at-me stuff. They post the good family pictures.

No one is going to make an Instagram post about having an affair. No one is going to post about their broken relationship with their parents or siblings. People will generally not post about how much they hate their job. And they rarely, if ever, post about how they are falling apart inside.

But they will post the pretty, polished parts. So don't fall for the trap. If you do all the urgent stuff and someday you get to the same position that person is in, you might just find it is a messy, complicated existence you want no part of.

Trust me in this. I have played the comparison and jealousy game plenty. And there is a reason the word lousy is in jealousy. It never works out the way you think it might. You find the skeletons in someone else's closet, and what you thought looked so amazing from a distance really looks vaguely like a turd when you are aware of the whole story.

Seriously, this is really a good place to start. If we ditch the comparisons, we will be in a good place going forward. Think of how much better things could be if we didn't want what he or she has and could find a path to contentment where we are at?

So there's a start, but how do we begin to kick the false sense of urgency and its mascots, the four horsemen, out of our lives? Well, I am guessing if you are still with me at this point of the book, you have an awareness of your own struggles with the false sense of urgency. I really think everyone struggles with it to some extent. And since I am not naive enough to realize you will forget the vast majority of what you have read here, I'd like to offer an acronym to help you remember a few things. After all, we need a plan to kick this thing in the teeth once and for all—or at least do our best to give it the ol' heave-ho.

Since we are talking about the false sense of urgency, let's use URGENCY as our acronym:

Unplug. I know this will be hard for some, nearly impossible for others. I will be honest. This is hard for me. I struggle with this, and I am keenly aware of it. Our brains need to be unplugged—unplugged from TV, from phones, from computers, from tablets. It needs some time for refreshing. It needs some decluttering time. It needs some healing time, without so many distractions. This one is nonnegotiable, in my opinion. And if we never unplug, there may not be any headspace or processing space even to tell Houston we have a problem.

Recognize the problem. Are you scurrying around from this to that at a frantic pace and seem to get nothing done? Are you constantly feeling as if there is an infinite amount of things to do but you don't even know where to start? Does life constantly feel out of order and chaotic? Do you feel as if you have absolutely no margin? Does it take you days to unwind on a vacation, or do you leave the house in full vacation mode? Are you someone who has calculated the number of weekends you have left until your kids graduate or move out of the house and then let the anxiety of that overwhelm you? Trust me in this: all this comes to light when you have to sit in the reality of it for a while, or even a moment. So sit in it. Ponder it. It is okay that there is a problem. As GI Joe used to say, "Now you know. And knowing is half the battle."

Game plan. What will I do differently when I recognize myself getting caught in the trap of the false sense of urgency? Will I attack it head-on, or will I take a more passive approach and tune out the voices by leaning into my identity, knowing who I am, and knowing my truth? Either of these approaches can be effective. Attacking it leads to getting things done and then stepping away when those things are done. And make sure you are focusing on the important things, the things that will matter in time, managing the tasks on your plate and then discarding the plate so it cannot bother you anymore, at least until it gets refilled. A more passive approach is simply deciding which tasks are important and realizing who you are and that you are better than someone who gets trapped under an impossible load of who-knows-what. Tell the false sense to go jump in the lake.

Escape from those things that are filling your life with urgency. I do not mean to run and hide in fear, but if a grizzly bear is chasing me, I want to escape, or the result will be bad. An accurate assessment of the activities and things you are involved with is in order. Are there volunteer obligations, committees, boards, or a job or friendships that are sucking the life out of you? If you are volunteering for something and you dread it whenever you think about it, do you really need that kind of stress? Can you break away? Are you way overcommitted? Here is the reality: you can hold me to this. You do *not* have to volunteer for every committee, coach all of your kids' sports teams, be on seven nonprofit boards, and have a full-time job and hope to have any level of peace in the midst of all of that. This is just reality. If I just described you, *you need to simplify.* Talk with one of your trusted advisors, and have them help you decide what needs to go. Make sure everything you are committed to has your best *yes*. That means if you commit to something, you commit to it. You are in. Not half in but fully in. And you can only have so many things that you are fully in. If they don't have your best yes, you need to trim. You get one shot at this life. Do not overcommit yourself to an early death or to the death of relationships because you have no time. And if you are the opposite and your false sense of urgency comes from being bored and not having enough to do, find something to do! There are so many volunteer opportunities. So many people with jobs they don't love have found life balance by adding volunteer opportunities that give them joy. Or find a hobby. Find things that occupy your time and give you joy.

There is a start: unplug, recognize, game plan, escape. Now, as those things happen and you realize their importance in your life, you can finish out the word with NCY.

Name the things that are important to get done. Name the things that are actually worthy of your time. Not everything gets to make the cut here. You don't have to do everything for everyone. You do not have to be everything for everyone, and you can't. It's just not possible. A great friend calls it "managing expectations." The people I know who are the most consumed by the false sense of urgency are the same people who simply cannot say no—to anyone. They race around doing everything for everyone and end up with entitled kids and spouses who know everything will just be handled for them. Sometimes, the answer to others is just "No, I can't do that for you." Again, please give your best yes, or it has to be no. You owe this to yourself! Life has to be sustainable. Overloading yourself to the point of breakdown is simply not sustainable.

Checklist. In aviation, checklists are everything. Aviation checklists were born out of, you guessed it, airplane crashes. They are one way to avoid plane crashes, and they are one way to avoid people crashes. Yes, that's a thing. I just made it up, but you know what I mean. One way to defeat the false sense of urgency is to make a list of the things running around in our heads. Make the list, and then prioritize and start checking things off! Prioritize according to importance. Delegate when you can. Remember, you can't do everything and shouldn't have to.

There are things and tasks that must be done now or today,

and there are also things that can wait awhile. So much urgency is created because we spend time checking off the this-can-wait list and push back or procrastinate doing the things that need to get done today. I am all for picking low-hanging fruit, but let's get done what needs to be done first.

And let's face it: not much is more satisfying (at least for me) than crossing things off a list when they are done and then ultimately throwing the list in the trash. Done. Finito. Buh-bye. Even the feeling of crossing things off the list is invigorating. One note: don't keep a tattered old checklist forever. Make a new one every couple of days. Some even make one each day so they can look at their day in a snapshot. Either is fine. Find out what works for you. This also keeps the list from getting stagnant. And if an item has been there for months, either do it or decide it doesn't need to be done! Re-prioritize your list regularly so you can see what the new important items are.

Yes! Yes because you did it! Give yourself a little credit! This isn't a cheesy, better-add-one-more-letter-to-finish-this thing. It is true. You are one step closer to kicking the false sense of urgency to the curb for good and freeing yourself up to really focus, being present for what really matters.

Be honest with yourself, and extend yourself some grace. Shame and condemnation are never productive and really do not help. Make a checklist. Make an accurate checklist with actual priority levels. You can make your own priority system. I like to use stars or all caps to designate importance on my list. And listen to me here: if you flub it up and do not get it all done, there is always tomorrow (unless the deadline is tonight, in which case, get that thing knocked out). Urgent things are okay, and life is full of them, but don't make an urgency out of the other things.

Do what brings you joy and pays the bills. Unfortunately, you really need to do both, have joy and pay the bills. I have also heard it said this way- make enough money in your job so you can do things that bring joy outside of work. My son, Blake, met with a "college whisperer," as we called her during his junior year of high school. The goal was to find out what he might want to do with his life, or at least find some direction. Blake met with her for ninety minutes, and then Amy and I returned for ninety more minutes of discussion amongst the four of us. Blake had contemplated being a dentist. I sensed all along that this was not the right fit for him, but I didn't want to squash that dream if it wasn't meant to be. Some of the first words out of Ramona's mouth when we were all together were, "He doesn't have a dental bone in his body." It was true. Dentistry was not a good fit for Blake. Better to find out then! She also talked about finding something Blake enjoyed that also paid the bills and paid off college debt. Blake had thought he liked the idea of being a dentist, but that was just it: he liked the *idea*, but it certainly isn't a good fit for him as he doesn't enjoy science classes. So we had some discussions about some possible avenues for Blake, and it was incredible. Ramona discussed how the word passion is thrown around and how many passionate people we have out there who are still searching for something to do. It's about more than just passion.

My reality is that I have nothing to fall back on. I never achieved an undergraduate degree. I am qualified to be a dentist. That's it. So for now, it is dentistry for me, but it doesn't have to be. It could be something else that affects the lives of others and is all about relationships (the things that bring me the most joy).

If you are totally stuck in a job you hate or dread or have anxiety about, but you feel that you have to keep that job, how can you make it better? Can you handle your responsibilities differently? Can you make a difference in your coworkers' lives? What can you do to make the job different and more enjoyable for you? Then act on it. And always count the cost of what you are proposing. But be prepared to leap! Little inputs can make a big difference. Something as simple as a new mantra or personal vision statement can make you see life through a different lens.

Maybe it is as easy as focusing on what you get to do instead of what you have to do. You get to work. What about the millions who are unemployed, many of whom would really like the chance to work? You have that chance. How can you make the most of it? And if it is the absolutely wrong fit, then explore your options. Can you learn a new skill? Can you go back to school? What inputs can you make to change your situation to a more favorable one?

And if you are someone who finds yourself without a job, maybe now is the time to pursue that next thing, the time to become marketable, the time to consider a pivot or a switch. It's a hard time for you, no doubt about that, but what could come from it? Maybe something better than you could imagine.

And what about all this stuff we are chasing? What is the end game? When will we be happy? How much is enough? Does our stuff bring us joy? And if we are being honest with ourselves, will that next thing we are chasing bring us any joy, or will it just bring us debt and responsibility? Does the new and shiny handcuff us with bills and credit card payments?

If your stuff didn't own you, would you have less urgency and more contentment? How hard do you really want to work just to pay for your house, cars, toys, vacation homes, vacations, and hobbies? If some of those things were simplified, could you work less or be less stressed? Just a thought. Again, count the cost of all these things we "need" to have.

So find what makes you happy and brings you joy, and do a lot of that. Seek to find contentment, that place where happiness and joy intersect. Make others' lives better, and in doing so, those people will help make your life better.

Put down your phone, please. The answers are not all in there, no matter how hard you look. Sit in total quiet for a few (or a lot of) minutes. Let your brain install its updates and rest and recover. Watch the sunrise or sunset. Take it all in. Let yourself rest. Be the best you. Not the best someone else, the best you. You got this. You were not an accident. You are here on purpose. You are here for a purpose. And we get this life to figure out that purpose.

This life is about moments. And the false sense of urgency steals moments in favor of the tyranny of the urgent. It doesn't allow for moments, because it is too busy trying to feed the horses or to get you to move onto the next thing, the next urgency—when you clean and organize over and over again and never have anyone else to help you enjoy it, when your mind says you have 8 million things to do but you go to make a list and there are really only a few important things, but your mind tells you otherwise.

We have to tame the false sense if we want to have moments. Are you willing to just drop everything and have a conversation or some much-needed playtime with your kids or your spouse or friend and go for ice cream? Or are you constantly scrambling with busywork that makes it appear you just had a productive day?

Will it matter in five minutes, five hours, five weeks, five months, or five years? Is it a busy list item or a trajectory item? Remember, busy list items are done out of perceived obligation. Maybe they don't have to be done right now. These are wants or perceived busyness. You all know someone who is trapped in this. Maybe it is you? Trajectory items are more important and may actually affect your trajectory. Better get these knocked out.

This is your life. Yes, it will go faster than you think—sometimes not the hours, but definitely the days, weeks, months, and years. Try listening to the song "100 Years," by Five for Fighting, and try to keep a straight face without crying as you really hear the lyrics. One day, we are graduating from high school. In a blink, we are married. Next blink, our kids are in school. Then they graduate, we retire, grandkids, and it all goes so fast. We simply must live in the moment if we want to enjoy this life and crush the false sense of urgency. We owe it to ourselves, and we owe it to those we are with to be 100 percent present, to be totally there with them, not mentally on to the next thing.

Don't wish it all away. Don't always be living for the next weekend, which will come and go at lightning speed. What can you do today to bless someone else? How can you make today count? What might make today different? What could you do that will cause you to lay your head on the pillow tonight with a big smile and a sense of satisfaction?

Life just catches up to you sometimes. Running too hard, too fast, for too long eventually results in a crash, especially if you run urgently. It just isn't sustainable. I pray you figure that out by choice before the crash, because the crash will take you out!

Do not stop and feed the horses, at least the four horses we have talked about. They already follow you around, waiting for an opportunity. Don't give them anything. Teach them that they will get no table scraps from you. Tell them to run along. You aren't available. Remember who you are and your importance in the world. Grab ahold of this thing called life with both hands. Remember, you only get one shot. Make it count.

And one last point here: gratitude and the four horsemen can not exist in the same space. Gratitude slows down life and tells the false sense to get lost. Urgency goes against gratitude and contentment. Thankfulness elevates us above the horses. Griping and whining takes us back down. We have a lot to be thankful for. Take some time to ponder what you have and not what you don't have. Be thankful. It helps!

Chapter 18

#WINTHENOW

Win the now. Win where you are at
right now. And then win the next thing.
And keep on going. One thing at a
time. And then you will win the day.

—*Eric Recker*

Here is one last chance to grab your attention before this book is put down in favor of whatever is next. And if you remember one thing in your quest to help defeat the false sense of urgency, please remember this. It is really important. So here is the reminder I want to leave you with that I hope runs circles in your mind for years to come:

Win the Now
#WINtheNOW

Why win the now? Because now is what we have. What is right in front of us is what we were designed for. Right here, right now. Fully present, not fully distracted by our devices and other stuff. Just right now. Tomorrow is important. What I am doing next is important. The other things running around in my mind are important. There is no doubt about that. And we need to plan the best we can, but we must hold on to tomorrow's plans a bit loosely. What happens next may need to wait a bit. Those things may not happen. If COVID-19 has shown us anything, it's that things may change. And they do change even without COVID-19.

What is certain is what is right in front of you! I had a perfect example of this just a few days ago. I drove up to meet a friend in Minneapolis. It was the halfway point for us to meet. It was fantastic to meet up, and we had a great discussion. We talked about relationships and being business owners and all the distractions we face in a given day. We both dislike our phones but know they are necessary devices in our culture today. Being connected is important. But we also talked about how others in our lives sometimes don't understand our connectedness and our availability for others. They feel as if we are distracted. And let's be honest, we are. But there is nothing more important than what is in front of us. Or next to us on the couch. Or at the same table for dinner. Or playing a game with us. So we discussed strategies to be fully present and to take a break, if necessary, to deal with an urgent issue on the phone.

What simply can't happen is halfway presence in the moment and halfway presence on the phone. You end up doing neither well. We can't multitask. We all know it. We discussed it before. It is a lie. And you sure can't multitask relationships.

Urgency tells us that stress, worry, fear, and anxiety about tomorrow and the next thing are all okay and perfectly acceptable. Urgency says we have to do all this stuff and have our minds be preoccupied and busy and scattered. If worries about the next thing in the cue for the day are out of the equation, we can win the now.

Win the now crushes the false sense of urgency because the false sense is all about what is next. It is all about what you haven't yet done and need to do. If you are present in the now, the false sense has no power!

Win the now by making a list of what needs to be done and checking off that list systematically until you can pitch it. This sets you up for success.

Win the now by adding value to someone else's life, by making their moment or moments with you, their now, better. By paying it forward. By buying someone else's coffee. By giving someone a smile. By showing up for them. By sending a random handwritten note of encouragement. By speaking compliments. By looking them in the eyes. By not being distracted. By using body language that tells them you have time for them and they matter.

You may be the only one who behaves that way toward them. What if your being present in the now for someone else makes all the difference in the world for them? What if it changes their trajectory for the better. What if they truly need your undivided attention and you give it to them? Wow. How cool would that be? So let the phone ring. Ignore the text until an appropriate time to step away. Whoever sent it will be fine. They aren't right in front of you. If they keep calling and texting, then maybe there is a problem.

And while we are discussing it, set appropriate boundaries.

If everyone who messages you or calls you gets an immediate response, then that is what they will expect. But if that is happening, I imagine a few things are getting pushed off to the side in favor of the phone. Let people know how important they are to you when they are in front of you. Be like Stan! Win the now!

Win the now for others, and you win the now for yourself! The winner of right now is the one who helps others realize and achieve their dreams. And if you win the now, chances are you will win the day! And that's amazingly cool!

I started writing this chapter as win today. But for me, a day is too big. I have too many interactions in a day. Between patients and staff and my family, it can be a really big number. And if a day is my metric, then I am in trouble because some of those interactions will be good and some will be bad. If my whole day hinges on all of those interactions being great, I set myself up for failure. But I still try to win each one for the person I am in front of.

I mean, think about it. How good does it feel to be heard? How good does it feel to hear someone say your name? How good does it feel to be around someone who cares? Contrast that to the person who is scrolling through their phone while you are talking with them and gives you a casual uh-huh here and there. How important does that make you feel?

So nail that presentation because you are fully there. Nail breakfast with your family because you are dialed in and not mentally out the door already. Nail the bedtime book-reading time with the kids because they deserve it. Nail the time of deleting and responding to emails because that is also important.

Why not win the now in hopes of winning today? And remember, today has twenty-four hours, and you get to use around sixteen of those hours. At the beginning of the first college semester, I was having a conversation with Blake about prioritizing all the activities he is involved in this fall. And we talked about which activities are worthy of his sixteen hours.

When he looked at it from that perspective and his desire to win the now, he knew that wasn't possible if he is overloaded. So he did some subtraction to make sure he can be fully present in each of his activities.

Also, give yourself some grace. If you do not win the now and it goes differently than you had hoped, you can try again. Pick yourself back up and give it another try. Don't believe the lies. The urgency is a lie. Baloney. You don't need it in your lives. Trust me.

I am a phone checker. Unchecked, I would probably pick the thing up a hundred times in a day. That is no secret. But a few weeks ago, we had some friends over for dinner and to watch a football game. These friends are not phone checkers. After a conversation with Amy, we agreed my phone would stay safely out of reach, with the volume on a bit just in case there was an important notification.

Spoiler alert: How often are our notifications really all that important? Sure, a patient could call who had an accident with a tooth, but that happens about once a year, so that's not a good enough excuse. We trick ourselves into thinking there will be something important that we can't miss, or we simply have FOMO (fear of missing out).

That night was so freeing! I didn't pick up my phone—at all. I checked it after my friends had left and Amy and I had talked a bit. But the point is this: I missed nothing, and I was fully present. I won the now, and it felt good. Could I have still had a great night if I checked my phone a few times? Sure, but that's not the point. Win the now. Be there. Fully there. People will be fine if they get a delayed response.

So what might this look like for a stay-at-home mom with little ones, who is overwhelmed by task and caring for kids who need attention and a lot of it? First, breathe. Breathe a lot. Lots of deep breaths through the day. You don't descend from the lineage of Wonder Woman or Superman, and you simply can't do it all. Get one thing done at a time, focus on that thing, and then move on to the next. And take a little time to be present with those little ones, who will be all grown up in the blink of an eye. Please, give yourself a little grace. The tasks will still be there tomorrow, and dinner may look like takeout.

For the CEO whose head is spinning in a million places in the year that is 2021, be present 100 percent in your current meeting. Make great lists for whatever is next so those things get out of your head so you can be present. Then fully move onto the next thing. I know that a ton may be riding on tomorrow's big meeting—it may be the meeting of the year—but that doesn't mean that until then, everyone else deserves your second best. One thing at a time, giving your best, being present and undistracted (as much as that is possible).

For the college student preparing for finals: Do one thing at a time. Don't wait until the last minute, or you won't give yourself your best and you won't win. And please, take some time to eat and rest. You got this. It's unlikely your whole life rests on the results of one test.

For the dentist or MD or chiropractor or cosmetologist or therapist moving from one patient or one client to the next, win the now for the one who is in front of you right now. Be fully there. The next one may have to wait, but that is okay. You are one person. And create the kind of culture that says, "I will give you my best, but first, I must give this person my best." Recharge. You can't give out of what you don't have to give. Rest. Breathe. Exercise. Take care of yourself.

For the waiter or waitress or person working at the checkout counter in a store, what is most important? The person or table right in front of you. Win that interaction, and then be ready for the next one, and get in the habit of taking a deep breath before you move on to the next table or check the next person out. Oxygen is therapeutic, and a deep breath is cleansing.

Especially in our current culture, people need our best. They need us to be firing on all cylinders as much as we can. People need to be noticed. They need to be made to feel important. They need to be called by name. There is tremendous power in saying someone's name. You may be the only human interaction they have all day, so make it a good one!

Win the now. Win each moment. Stack those wins on top of each other and take a few losses. Then realize that even the best coaches and managers and players never had a perfect record. In baseball, 20 wins and 6 losses added up over multiple seasons get you into the Hall of Fame every single time. You won't be perfect. You will stumble. You will fall. You will fail. And people will fail you. But try. Do your best. Win the now.

God has given us a whole bunch of moments, a whole bunch of "nows," but His real gift to us is the present—that which is right in front of us. So win the present, the moment He has given us. And just for fun, watch the effect it has on others.

Winning the now is all about presence, so you may need to do some self-discovery and self-awareness to see the things that are stealing your ability to be present and to make some tough choices, like Blake did. If your entire day, you are chaotically running from one thing to the next, barely giving any of it your best, you may be overloaded. You can't be fully present and win the now if you are overloaded. It may be time to simplify.

Don't let the false sense of urgency rob you of the moments that give your life flavor and meaning in exchange for what might be someday. Because someday may not come. So many things can happen to affect the future, but we do have now.

To provide a daily reminder, we will be making bracelets that say #WINtheNOW. They will be available for purchase on my website. You can find me at www.ericrecker.com Pick up a few and give them to others and share the message. I feel it can be life changing.

The bracelets are not a way to pad my pocket. The proceeds for these bracelets will be going to Many Hands for Haiti, a group that is helping Haitians become better today so they can have a more healthy and productive tomorrow. Check out their website, mh4h.org. Good stuff!

So WIN the NOW!

For yourself

For others

For Haitians

A few things to end on:

I just finished up a weekend retreat at Wildwood Hills Ranch in St. Charles, Iowa, with my fellow board members for Many Hands for Haiti, and I wanted to share this quote from the executive director. Wildwood Hills Ranch is a place where every child matters. Their goal is to transform lives and strengthen communities. Matt Moeckl told me that they were there to "love them enough to meet them right where they are at and love them enough to not leave them there."

That about sums it up. As we encounter people in this life in an attempt to #WINtheNOW, for them and for us, we need to love them right where they are. And we need to have the courage to love them enough to not leave them there. If we do that, we are all elevated and become better versions of ourselves, and the world becomes a better place!

Bibliography

1. https://q92hv.iheart.com/content/2019-01-29-these-are-americas-top-10-fears/)

2. (https://www.washingtonpost.com/news/wonk/wp/2014/10/30/clowns-are-twice-as-scary-to-democrats-as-they-are-to-republicans/)

3. (https://www.nbcnews.com/better/pop-culture/praise-worry-why-fretting-can-be-good-you-ncna757016)

4. (https://www.psychologytoday.com/us/blog/think-act-be/201907/how-often-do-your-worries-actually-come-true)

5. (https://www.cdc.gov/media/releases/2016/p0215-enough-sleep.html#:~:text=35%25%20of%20U.S.%20adults%20are%20not%20getting%20the,and%20Prevention%E2%80%99s%20%28CDC%29%20Morbidity%20and%20Mortality%20Weekly%20Report.)

6. (https://news.gallup.com/poll/5314/Eyes-Wide-Open-Americans-Sleep-Stress.aspx#:~:text=Another%2055%25%20of%20Americans%20report%20getting%20either%20six,hour%20less%20than%20what%20Gallup%20measured%20in%201942.)

7. (https://www.sleepfoundation.org/articles/why-electronics-may-stimulate-you-bed)